Colorado West

LAND OF GEOLOGY

AND WILDFLOWERS

by
Robert G. Young and Joann W. Young

Published by
Robert G. Young
P.O. Box 40743
Grand Junction, Colorado 81501

Printed in the United States of America by
Artistic Printing Co.
Salt Lake City, Utah

Library of Congress Catalog Card No.: 83-60836
ISBN 0-9611010-0-8

FOREWORD

This book is designed as a guide to the most common wildflowers and the general geology of that portion of Colorado west of the continental divide. In this region there are many more varieties of wildflowers than described herein; but we have selected the more widespread and showy kinds which are most likely to attract the reader's attention. Likewise, the geology could be treated in more detail; but we believe the amateur would likely lose interest in a lengthy discourse.

To aid the amateur in recognizing plants and geologic features, we have included as many illustrations as is econimically feasible. Most of the drawings and photos were produced by the writers, but we wish to express our gratitude to Winifred Bull for the use of the lady slipper photo and to Debbie Higley for the numerous artistic sketches which lend a touch of humor to the book.

J.W.Y.
R.G.Y.

Colorado West

CONTENTS

ILLUSTRATIONS

GEOLOGY OF
Colorado West

THE BIG PICTURE

In order to set the stage for the more detailed treatises on each of the major physiographic regions of Colorado West, it seems necessary to describe the region as a whole. This vast area embracing that portion of Colorado west of the Continental Divide, is truly a land of beauty and contrasts. Its beauty lies in the magnificent handiworks of nature which seem to abound on every side—the mountains cloaked in rich shades of green to brown and topped-off by jagged snow-capped peaks of the higher ranges, the varicolored and intricately sculptured cliffs casting their shadows across the desert lowlands or upon well-watered valleys at their bases, and the seemingly endless variety of wildflowers occupying specific habitats ranging from the lowest desert valley to the highest barren mountain top.

As for the contrasts, they too can be most pleasing. The lowest point in Colorado (about 4,300 feet) occurs where the Colorado River crosses into Utah; whereas, less than 100 miles distant, numerous peaks in the West Elk and San Juan Mountains stretch more than 14,000 feet into the sky. Large portions of Colorado West consist of low-lying regions of sparse vegetation which qualify as deserts, inasmuch as they receive less than 10 inches of moisture per year. However, with a moderate rise in elevation and a concomitant increase in precipitation, the vegetation becomes noticeably more lush until ultimately, in the montane areas, the ground is generally covered with a verdant cover of trees and lush grass reflecting moisture amounts up to 40 inches per year. The population density, too, shows pronounced imbalance. Nearly all the metropolitan areas, with their halos of intensive agriculture, are clustered along the few rivers and major creeks. The remaining more remote portions of Colorado West, however, serve as home for a much smaller number of farmers, ranchers, miners and other residents, who, either by choice or necessity, have elected to cast their lot in the less crowded areas.

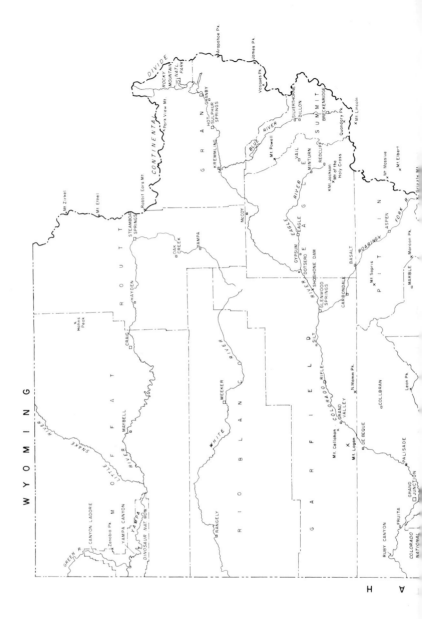

Fig. 1 Location Map of Colorado West

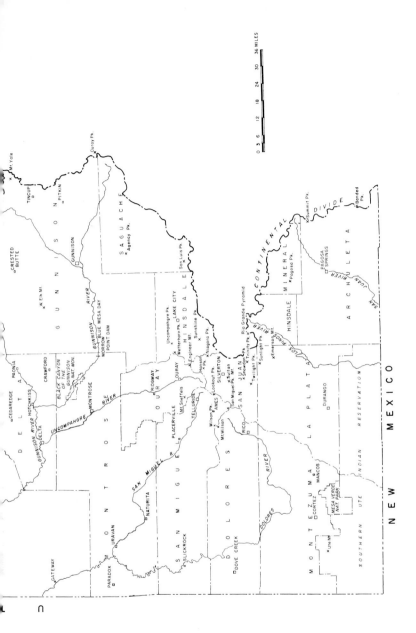

15

Because of its great range in elevations, Colorado West offers a variety of humidity and temperature conditions. In winter, snow may blanket the entire region for brief periods but tends to linger and accumulate to greater depths at the higher elevations, much to the delight of the skiing enthusiasts for whom numerous runs and facilities have been constructed. Many of the lower valleys have relatively mild winters and are literally crowded with apple, pear, peach and cherry orchards which supply much of the fruit for Colorado and surrounding states. During the long summers temperatures may soar to more than 100°F. in the valleys and desert areas; but one can quickly escape this sometimes oppressive heat by retreating to one of the nearby mountain areas where increased elevation is accompanied by a welcome decrease in temperature.

Rather than burden the reader with a list of stream and place names, we have prepared an index map depicting the major features of Colorado West. Physiographers, those who differentiate between major physical features of the Earth's surface, generally agree that Colorado West includes portions of four major physiographic divisions—the Central Rocky Mountains, Southern Rocky Mountains, Wyoming Basins and Colorado Plateau Provinces. These provinces can be further subdivided into some 19 smaller areas each of which is topographically distinct. Each of these areas is the subject of a separate discussion in a later section of this book. Before doing so, however, it seems appropriate to introduce the reader to the geologic history of the area.

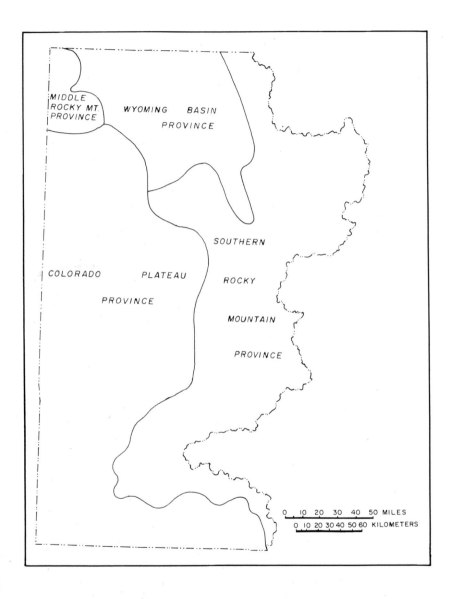

MIDDLE
ROCKY MT.
PROVINCE

WYOMING   BASIN
PROVINCE

SOUTHERN

COLORADO   PLATEAU   ROCKY
PROVINCE
MOUNTAIN
PROVINCE

0   10   20   30   40   50 MILES
0   10 20 30 40 50 60 KILOMETERS

Figure 2—Physiographic provinces of Colorado West

SETTING THE STAGE

Although Colorado West does not contain every type of geo-logic feature known to man, it does have a great variety, not the least of which are its numerous types of rocks—sedimentary, intrusive igneous (plutonic), extrusive igneous (volcanic) and metamorphic (older rocks altered by heat and pressure). Most of the rocks we find exposed at the surface in this region show well-defined layering or bedding. These are primarily sedimen-tary rocks, which formed incredibly long ago in or on long-vanished deserts, floodplains, swamps, lakes, beaches or even shallow seas. Some of the layers contain fossilized remains of organisms; whereas, others contain radioactive minerals, both of which assist us in assigning an age to them and enable us to place them in an orderly succession or time framework, as shown in the stratigraphic columns for each of the regions. A glance at these columns will reveal that the approximately five billion years of Earth's history can be divided into four *eras* (Precambrian, Paleozoic, Mesozoic and Cenozoic) and that each *era* is divided into two or more *periods*. These *periods*, most of which lasted for tens of millions of years, are one of the most useful time units for the geologist. It is also worth noting that the rocks formed during a *period* are referred to as a *system*.

Sedimentary rocks in Colorado West range in age from Cambrian to Quaternary; but as seen in the various columns, rocks present in some areas may be absent in others and one system (Silurian) is entirely missing in this region.

In higher areas, such as the San Juan or West Elk Mountains, layered rocks of a different kind may catch your eye. These are volcanic rocks such as lavas, tuffs and breccias; products of eruptions which occurred here in the Tertiary Period.

In other places, especially where streams have carved deeply into uplifted areas, erosion has revealed extremely ancient basement rocks of metamorphic and intrusive igneous origin. The intrusive igneous rocks (granites, diorites, gabbros, etc.) are formerly molten rocks which invaded older rocks from below and then cooled before reaching the surface. Some of the rocks into which they were forced show very little change, but

18

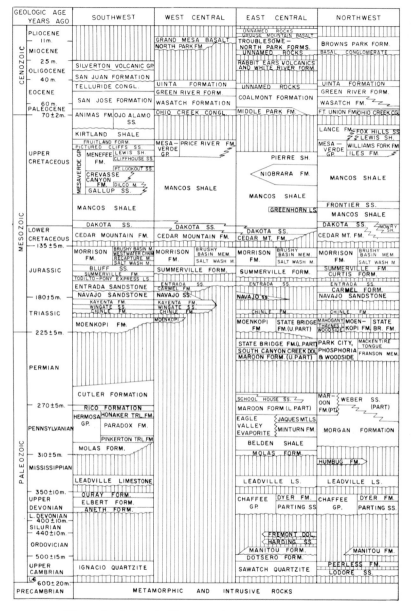

Figure 3—Colorado West stratigraphic correlation chart

19

others were distorted and partially recrystallized by these and other disturbances to form metamorphic rocks such as slate, phyllite, schist, gneiss, quartzite, etc. The metamorphic rocks are mostly Precambrian; whereas, the intrusives are Precambrian, Cretaceous and Tertiary.

Nearly all sedimentary rocks are deposited in layers or beds which are roughly horizontal, but with time the surface of the Earth undergoes marked changes. Much of the crust has been subjected to titanic forces which form upfolds (anticlines, domes and monoclines), downfolds (synclines and basins) or faults (fractures along which a block of crust moves differentially with respect to another block). In other places the emplacement of molten rock from below has domed up or otherwise distorted the overlying strata or layers of rock. Commonly these injections cooled beneath the surface to form batholiths, laccoliths, stocks, dikes and sills of relatively coarse-grained crystalline intrusive rock, but in a few places they reached the surface where they escaped from volcanic vents as lava flows, cinders, ash and dust. These later cooled or became consolidated to form basalts, breccias and tuffs. Some of these volcanoes were merely large fractures from which poured huge volumes of lava, but others built cones of cinders or combinations of cinders and flows and had craters at their summits. When volcanic activity ceased, some volcanoes were quickly dissected by erosion with the cone being completely removed by action of wind and water, leaving only a vertical plug of congealed basaltic material marking the throat or feeder pipe of the old volcano. In the San Juan Mountains, cessation of volcanic activity was commonly marked by collapses of a broad area around a volcano to form a collapse caldera or huge crater some 10 to 15 miles in diameter. Sometimes a new volcano would rise within a caldera, form a large cone, then collapse to form a caldera within a caldera.

Other regions of the Earth's surface may have as wide a spectrum of rocks and geologic structures as those occurring in Colorado West, but what makes this region outstanding are the remarkable exposures of its rocks. The outcrops of Mesozoic and Cenozoic sedimentary rocks in the Book Cliffs and Roan Cliffs along the southern edge of the Uinta Basin are truly spectacular and are unexcelled. Here the strata are unobscured by vegetation or weathering products, they stand in nearly vertical cliffs many hundreds of feet high and one can trace individual sandstone, shale or coal layers for many miles.

On Minerals and Fuels:

Metals and Nonmetals: — Colorado West has been referred to as a minerals and fuels storehouse, and this is truly so. First to be exploited were its treasure of precious metals (gold and silver) locked in their strong boxes of stone high in the forbidding valleys and peaks of such lofty regions as the San Juan, Elk, Sawatch and Park Ranges. In the late 1860's and early 1870's a number of gold and silver deposits of considerable importance were discovered in such places as Hahns Peak, Summitville, Lake City, Rosita, Silverton, Ouray, Aspen and Tin Cup. Commonly associated with the precious metals are lesser ones such as lead, zinc and copper (base metals) which have been and still are being mined in sizeable quantities. The mining of not-so-glamorous nonmetals such as fluorospar, barite, gypsum, limestone and sand and gravel also began with the arrival of the earliest white settlers, and dollarwise their value has undoubtedly far exceeded that of the metals produced.

Coal: — The first fuel to be utilized in this region by white settlers was most likely wood, but before many days had passed numerous small coal mines were in operation. The local demand for coal increased steadily until the 1940's when many industries switched to the use of petroleum. After three decades of reduced demand, production of coal is again rising toward a new high; and operators are beginning to tap the huge coal reserves of Colorado West by open pit and underground methods. It has been calculated that there are 145 billion tons of mineable bituminous coal under less than 3,000 feet of overburden in this region.

Petroleum:—Petroleum was first discovered in Colorado West in 1830 at White River Dome west of Meeker; and shallow production was encountered in 1902 at Rangely, which was destined to become Colorado's largest field with discovery of deeper production in the 1930's. Sporadic exploration continued until the 1940's when search efforts increased many fold, and has continued at a relatively high rate until the present. Cumulative production to 1976 from Colorado West has been approximately one trillion cubic feet of natural gas and 500 million barrels of oil.

Oil Shale:—Another type of fuel present in the Piceance Creek basin is shale oil, locked in a dense brown banded rock referred to as oil shale, but which is actually a magnesium-rich marl containing kerogen, an immature hydrocarbon. This shale, which in places is more than 1,000 feet thick, formed in a shallow lake which covered most of the northern half of Colorado West in Eocene time, some 60 million years ago. Since that time, the old lake deposits have been uplifted and the margins of the basin dissected by erosion revealing the thin edge of the oil shale unit as a resistant unit near the top of the Roan Cliffs. The richest part of the oil shale at the outcrop is the Mahogany Ledge which yields as much as 50 gallons of oil per ton.

Enterprising pioneers distilled the shale to make axle grease for covered wagons and reportedly used it to heat peach orchards at Palisade and for other domestic purposes. The first retort was built in 1917 near DeBeque. Like many succeeding attempts, it was not a commercial success but did help to focus attention on this immense potential oil source. From that early beginning there have been periods of frantic activity separated by times of quiescence, reflecting changing economic conditions, introductions of new technologies or other less well defined incentives or deterrents. In recent years interest in developing new methods of recovery has increased with the result that operators are now beginning to recover a minute portion of the estimated one to three trillion barrels of petroleum locked in the Green River shales. Other products to be recovered with the petroleum include nahcolite (NaHCO3) and dawsonite [NaAl(OH)2CO3], of value for their sodium and aluminum content.

Uranium:—Another sought-after energy related mineral found in Colorado West is uranium (magic word of the atomic age!), used primarily to fuel our nuclear reactors. Uranium ore was first discovered in Jurassic rocks in Colorado West in 1879 by the Talbot brothers of Paradox. It was promptly forgotten but was rediscovered in 1897 to signal the beginning of the first uranium boom. This was the Radium Era which lasted until 1924. High grade uranium ore was shipped to Europe where it was processed for contained radium salts (radium is a daughter product of the atomic decay of uranium-238). During this period the United States produced' 200 grams of radium, valued at $100,000 per gram, and most of this came from the Uravan mineral belt of Colorado West.

The years 1924 to 1946 are referred to as the Vanadium Era. Much of the uranium ore in this region has associated with it varying amounts of vanadium, and since the value of radium had declined by that time, the ore was mined primarily for the vanadium which sold for

20 to 40 cents per pound of contained vanadium oxide.

In 1946 there began the next phase, the Uranium Era, brought about by the development of the atomic bomb. From that time until now, approximately 12 million tons of uranium-vanadium ore with a value of more than $500 million have been mined and milled in Colorado West. Most of the production has come from mines near Gateway, Uravan, Naturita, Slick Rock and Paradox in the Uravan mineral belt, but additional amounts have been mined from mines near Placerville, Maybell, Meeker, Gunnison, Rico and other localities.

Hydro-Electric:—One of our lesser used sources of energy is water power. A few of our rapidly flowing mountain streams have been harnessed for the generation of electricity. Such plants can be seen at Morrow Point Dam, Shoshone Dam and Ames.

Thermal Resources:—If we exclude Colorado West's abundant sunshine, the last of its major sources of energy is thermal. As you are probably aware, there is a steady rise in temperature with increasing depth below the earth's surface (geothermal gradient), but in some places temperatures are higher than normal near the surface because of recent volcanic activity or other factors. In other places large open fractures may penetrate to great depths, allowing ground waters to contact very hot rocks. In either situation ground waters become heated and rise toward the surface where they may escape as hot springs such as those at Steamboat Springs, Hot Sulfur Springs, Glenwood Springs, Pagosa Springs, Ouray and Ridgeway. Some day this source may contribute much to the energy needs of the regions.

SOME REALLY ANCIENT HISTORY

Any discourse on the geology of Colorado West would be less than complete if it did not review the sequence of events which have occured in this region from earliest recorded time to the present. Granted, we may have only a partial record of past events, but like patient detectives we are able to reconstruct a coherent picture from the clues preserved in the rocks. The task is made more complex by such factors as metamorphism (change of rocks from their original form by heat and pressure), diastrophism (folding and fracturing), paucity of fossils and lack of exposures. With this disclaimer we will now proceed with the probable history.

Earliest Times [Precambrian]—It is now fairly well agreed that the Earth was created from a clot of stellar dust about 4.5 to 4.8 billion years (b.y.) ago and that the first rocks formed about 3.8 b.y. ago. We are uncertain about what was happening during this time in Colorado West because the oldest rocks recognized here are some highly metamorphosed sediments found only along the northwest border of the State. They are dated at 2.5 b.y. and formed in the Wyoming Province during the Archean Era. Much more widespread are thick metamorphosed sediments and lava flows of the Churchill Province formed about 1.7 b.y. ago in the early Proterozoic Era. These are referred to variously as the Idaho Springs Formation, Black Canyon Schist, etc.

Intruded into these Early Proterozoic rocks are a number of igneous bodies such as the Vernal Mesa and Taylor Granites dated at about 1.4 to 1.48 b.y. ago. In a few places, somewhat younger (1.1 b.y.) and only slightly metamorphosed sediments overlie the older metamorphic and granitic rocks. One such unit is the Uncompahgre Formation exposed south of Ouray in the San Juan Mountains. All these younger rocks are considered to be Middle Proterozoic.

The Paleozoic Era [A Time of Abundant Primitive Life]:
—There is no record of Late Proterozoic sediments in Colorado West because none were formed, or, if they were, they were removed by subsequent erosion. In many areas Middle Proterozoic rocks are directly overlain by a much younger sequence of rocks formed during the Paleozoic Era which began about 600 million years (m. y.) ago. Thus between the two units there is a time gap or lacuna of at least 500 m.y. for which we have no rock record in this region.

The Paleozoic is divided into seven *periods* (or *systems* if we are discussing the rocks formed during these time periods) which are, from earliest to latest, the Cambrian, Ordovician, Silurian, Devonian, Mississippian, Pennsylvanian and Permian Periods.

Cambrian Period [Age of Trilobites]—This Era saw the rise and fall of many invertebrate groups and the beginnings of vertebrates which were to dominate the rest of geologic time. In Early and Middle Cambrian times, erosion apparently prevailed in this region because it stood somewhat above sea level as a part of the broad "Transcontinental Arch" extending southwestward from the Canadian Shield area in eastern Canada and crossing Colorado from north to south. Shallow seas advanced toward the crest of the Arch from both east and west and the western sea reached Colorado West in late Middle or early Late Cambrian time about 550 m.y. ago and eventually inundated most of this portion of the State. It also crossed the Transcontinental Arch via the "Colorado sag" and joined the eastern seas, thus dividing the Arch into a northern Siouxia uplift and a southern Sierra Grande uplift. Fossils are not common in these rocks but a few brachiopods and the segmented trilobites characteristic of the Cambrian, can be found.

Ordovician Period [Age of Graptolites]—Seas continued to cover most of Colorado West during Early Ordovician time but withdrew at the end of that Epoch. Middle and Upper Ordovician rocks occur in central Colorado but show evidence of temporary retreats of the eastern sea at the end of both Early and Middle Ordovician times. The eastern sea extended a short distance into Colorado West in both Middle and Late epochs leaving a thin record in the Sawatch Mountains. Cambro-Ordovician seas left behind as much as 1,000 feet of limestone, dolostone, shale and sandstone (which later became quartzite) when they finally withdrew. Though tiny colonial graptolites dominated Ordovician seas, their remains are few in Colorado West deposits. Trilobites, brachiopods and other forms are found, however.

Silurian Period [Age of Corals] —Silurian time seemingly was a time of erosion in Colorado West since no rocks of that age have been identified here. Actually, they are found in only one locality in Colorado, small patches north of Fort Collins in the northeastern part of the State. Because of this locality and their presence in adjacent states, it is likely that Silurian seas did cover at least a part of Colorado West but their products were later removed by erosion.

Devonian Period [Age of Fishes] —In late Devonian time a sea spread eastward from the Cordilleran trough in Utah to cover most or all of Colorado West. It moved in over a highly weathered and eroded terrain which provided much material for reworking and depositing in the shallow sea. When it withdrew westward at the end of the Period it left behind as much as 500 feet of limestone, dolostone, shale, and sandstone (which later became quartzite). Fossil brachiopods, corals, bryozoans, crinoids and clams are common in Colorado West but fish remains are relatively rare.

Mississippian Period [Age of Crinoids] —The disappearance of the sea at the end of the Devonian did not long endure. Soon after the beginning of Mississippian time, shallow seas again inundated Colorado from both east and west, eventually coalescing in the Colorado sag. These seas remained stationary during Early Mississippian time, withdrew for a brief period, then returned to cover the area for most of Late Mississipian time. In Colorado West, Mississippian time is recorded by as much as 600 feet of massive gray limestone and dolostone referred to as the Leadville, Madison or Red Wall Limestone. In northwestern Colorado, the Humbug Formation, with a thickness of about 100 feet, is present above the Leadville.

Near the end of Mississippian time, vigorous growth of two large northwest trending anticlinal uplifts began. These became the Colorado Mountains or ancestral Rocky Mountains which reached their greatest elevation in the Pennsylvanian and Permian Periods. These two great upwarps were Frontrangia (ancestral Front Range), in the general position of the Front Range, and Uncompahgria (ancestral Uncompahgre), encompassing the area now covered by the Uncompahgre uplift and the West Elk and San Juan Mountains. Separating the two uplifts was the Central Colorado trough and just to the west of Uncompahgria was the Paradox basin. Early growth of these structures was accompanied by retreat of the seas, so that latest Mississippian rocks are not recognized in Colorado West. Brachiopods and crinoid stems are the most common fossils of this unit in Colorado West.

Pennsylvanian Period [Age of Plants] —Subaerial weathering prevailed at the end of the Mississippian and the beginning of the Pennsylvanian resulting in a mature topography with some karst (cave development) in places. The weathering debris and soils of this period have been preserved as mostly red clastics. Near the end of Early Pennsylvanian time another shallow sea approached from the west and was beginning to lap at the flanks of the highlands. Limestones formed in the quiet waters of southwest and northwest Colorado while dark mudstones and shaly limestones accumulated in the two basins. By late Middle Pennsylvanian time Frontrangia and Uncompahgria had probably attained their maximum relief and the Central Colorado and Paradox basins had received great thicknesses of sediment. Thousands of feet of salt along with considerable arkose, black shale, limestone, dolostone, gypsum and anhydrite accumulated in the Paradox basin while lesser thicknesses of the same lithologies formed in the Central Colorado basin. The arkose represents coarse debris from the nearby highlands. In Late Pennsylvanian time, shallow marine limestone again predominated in southwestern Colorado, but large volumes of fine-grained red sediment were spread by streams through the Central Colorado basin and into northwestern Colorado where they mixed with a wind blown sand deposit forming in that area. In Colorado West, plant fossils

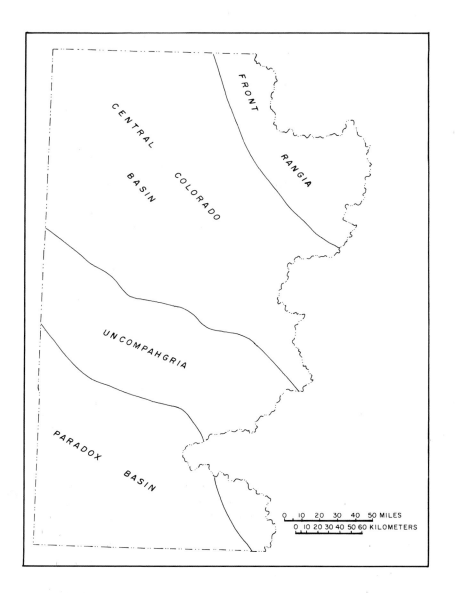

Figure 4—Ancestral Rocky Mountains of Colorado West

29

are rare but brachiopods, crinoids, pelecypods, gastropods, corals and bryozoans are relatively common.

Permian Period [Age of Fusulines]—In early Permian time the ancestral Rockies remained high and continued to shed coarse red sediment into the two basins. The sea had apparently withdrawn from all but the extreme northwest and southwest corners of Colorado West by the beginning of the Period. From then until the end of the Period, streams continued to wear down the highlands and spread the resulting debris across the Basins and beyond them to the north and west to intermix with the sand body still forming there. The sand appears to represent eolian (wind-blown) beach and shallow marine deposits related to the margin of a sea. In Middle Permian time the sea withdrew and weathering and erosion prevailed, but again the sea returned in Late Permian time. It entered only the northwest corner of Colorado where it deposited a thin limestone before retreating at the end of the Period. Wheat grain-shaped fusulinids (lime secreting protozoa), large pelecypods and strongly convex brachiopods are characteristic Permian fossils of this area.

The Mesozoic Era [Age of Reptiles]:—The next great subdivision of geologic time is the Mesozoic Era which can be subdivided into three periods—Triassic, Jurassic and Cretaceous. Land dwelling amphibians and reptiles had appeared in the late Paleozoic, but it was in the Mesozoic that they completely dominated the land. At times, Colorado West must have been home for hordes of reptiles, because their remains are abundant in some units exposed in this area.

Triassic Period—In early Triassic time a shallow sea approached from the west, stopped just after crossing into Colorado West and then withdrew leaving behind a wedge of thin-bedded red mudstones and even a bit of limestone in the northern part of the region. Erosion prevailed in Middle Triassic time but in the Late Triassic great masses of wind blown sand arrived from the northwest and these alternated with stream deposits from the south. These sediments lapped far up the flanks of the remnants of Uncompahgria but failed to cover them.

Large conifers and other plants grew on the floodplains and large dinosaurs and other reptiles left their tracks in the muds and sands, but their bones are rare.

Jurassic Period—During Early Jurassic time desert-like conditions appear to have prevailed. The evidence can be seen in the thick dune deposits common to the northern part of Colorado West. Middle Jurassic was a time of erosion in all but the northwest corner of Colorado, where some tidal flat deposits were formed. In Late Jurassic time desert conditions returned to Colorado West and produced a thick blanket of dune sand. Conditions moderated near the end of the Period as a shallow sea approached from the northwest. After a brief stay it retreated leaving behind beach sands, tidal flat muds, some gypsum and thin limestones. Following this, a layer of sand, mud and volcanic ash spread across the region from the southwest, recording mountain building in southern Arizona. On the Late Jurassic floodplains there flourished cycads, palms and conifers which served as food for hordes of dinosaurs of all sizes from a few inches to as much as 60 feet high. Their remains are common in the Morrison Formation.

Cretaceous Period—An erosional interval of seven to ten million years occurred in Colorado West at the end of the Jurassic and the beginning of the Cretaceous Period. Toward the end of this interval, mountain building (the Sevier orogeny) began in western Utah and eastern Nevada and simultaneously a great downwarp (the Rocky Mountain geosyncline) began to form in the position of the present Rocky Mountains. This colossal subsidence was hundreds of miles wide and extended from the Gulf of Mexico to Alaska. Its cause is uncertain but it appears to have been related to a subduction or down-dragged zone between two plates of the Earth's crust. Regardless of origin, it was quickly invaded by seas from north and south, which eventually commingled in southeastern Colorado. From there they spread westward and eastward over earlier floodplain deposits as the trough continued to sink. The sea, which we refer to as the Mancos sea in Colorado West, had inundated nearly all of Colorado by the end of Early Cretaceous time, reaching the Colorado-Utah line at just about that time. From here it continued to spread westward, reaching the old Sevier highland, and after a period of standstill there, began to recede eastward. By the end of the period it had withdrawn from nearly all of the geosyncline leaving behind deposits as much as two miles thick, consisting of shoreline sand and mud, shallow water marine muds and mixed types of floodplain sediments.

During the Cretaceous, a great variety of deciduous plants developed on the land and their remains are preserved as leaf, twig and stem impressions. But more important were the conifers which grew in swamps near the shore. Their remains accumulated in such thicknesses as to produce peat, which was later converted to bituminous coal. Dinosaurs roamed the land and left

their footprints in profusion in the coal swamps and coughed up their gizzard stones which accumulated in large numbers on the floodplains. In the sea lived the fish-like Icthyosaurs and other reptiles as well as numerous fishes, pelecypods, gastropods and cephalopods. Exoskeletons of the latter three types of animals are relatively common in the Mancos Shale of this area.

End of an Era: – At the end of the Cretaceous (and the Mesozoic Era) some 63 million years ago, all dinosaurs and flying reptiles disappeared from the land and air. Just why they died out so abruptly after dominating the world for 150 million years is a subject for speculation. One reasonable explanation is that widespread uplift and mountain building, which began in the Late Cretaceous and continued into the Tertiary, produced a colder climate and simultaneous changes in vegetation. If so, those cold-blooded forms could have starved or frozen to death. Another suggestion is that the more active warm-blooded mammals began to multiply rapidly and proceeded to make reptilian eggs and juvenile dinosaurs major items on their menus. It has also been postulated that they were eliminated by epidemic diseases or psychological stresses concomitant with overpopulation and limited food supplies. Other suggested causes include asteroid impacts and massive volcanic eruptions.

Not only were there changes in land reptiles at this time, but various marine types were also eliminated. Ammonite cephalopods and reptilian plesiosaurs, ichthyosaurs and mosasaurs all took their final bows at the end of the Era.

Destruction of a Geosyncline [Laramide Orogeny]: —The events which led to the many changes at the end of the Cretaceous are not fully understood; but they probably were the consequence of the convergence of two plates of the Earth's crust. It is believed that overriding of the Eastern Pacific (Farralon) plate by the American plate produced two imbricate subduction zones (zones where crust is dragged downward into the mantle). One zone was in eastern Nevada and west-

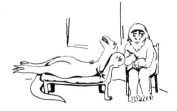

33

ern Utah, and the other was in Colorado West along the boundary between the Colorado Plateau and the Southern Rocky Mountains.

This event, which is usually referred to as the Laramide orogeny, began about 70 m.y. ago and continued for about 25 m.y., well into the Tertiary. Rocks in the geosyncline now began to wrinkle and fold in response to stresses related to the plate collision. Mountains began to rise as narrow, mostly north-south anticlines (upfolds) separated by broad subsiding basins and synclines (downfolds). The deformation appeared first in southwestern Colorado West, then spread northeastward. Some faulting (displacement along fractures) accompanied the folding and there was also some regional uplift which hastened the withdrawal of the sea.

A concurrent event was the intrusion of large masses of molten rock (batholiths) into the crustal rocks in two areas of Colorado West. These were the western side of the San Juan Mountains and the Elk Mountains-Sawatch Mountain area. Both batholiths formed within the Colorado mineral belt which had its inception at this time. The Colorado mineral belt contains the bulk of the mineral deposits in the State. Some of the molten rock managed to escape to the surface to form volcanic rocks in the San Juan Mountains, the San Juan basin and far to the north in Middle Park.

Mountains which appeared at this time were the renascent Uncompahgre uplift, together with the Needle Mountains, Elk Mountains, Sawatch Range, Park-Gore Range and Uinta

Mountains. Most of the basins had their beginnings at this time also. The Rocky Mountains were now a reality!

The Cenozoic Era [Mammals Take Over]: —When the Cenozoic began, the sea had disappeared from Colorado West for the last time and the only remaining reptiles were lizards, snakes, turtles, crocodiles and the like. They offered only token competition to the small but active primitive mammals who were destined to adapt to all environments, to increase greatly in size and numbers, and to dominate the world scene from that time forward.

The Cenozoic has been subdivided in various ways, but the most common division is into two periods—the Tertiary, lasting about 60 m.y. and the Quaternary, which has persisted for approximately 3 m.y. The Tertiary (Age of Mammals) is further divided into the Paleocene, Eocene, Miocene and Pliocene Epochs; whereas, the Quaternary (Age of Man) can be split into the Pleistocene (Ice Age) and the Holocene (Recent) Epochs.

Because events in Colorado West do not readily lend themselves to a detailed treatment by epochs, the Tertiary here is divided into early, middle and late portions.

Early Tertiary [Paleocene and Eocene Epochs]—As the Paleocene began, streams began to erode the crests of the growing mountains and to dump their loads into adjacent downwarped areas. Thousands of feet of rock were removed from the uplifts, commonly exposing Precambrian basement rocks. Simultaneously, the basin floors were being raised rapidly.

During late Paleocene and early Eocene times, the region remained just above sea level and the basins continued to receive stream transported sediments, including some volcanic debris from the uplifts. However, in middle Eocene time, small lakes in the basins of northern Colorado West and adjacent areas began to grow in response to increased rainfall and/or elevation. These lakes eventually coalesced to form one continuous lake—huge Green River Lake covering most of northeastern Utah, southwestern Wyoming and northwestern Colorado. One arm of the lake, called Uinta Lake, extended as far south as Grand Mesa. Some stream deposits accumulated around the Lake margins but most of the erosional products were dumped into the Lake. Here, the coarser fragments formed deltas, beaches and bars; whereas, the fines and dissolved materials were distributed by currents to all parts of the Lake to form shaly, marly or evaporitic deposits. Some geologists believe that the Lake waters were chemically stratified so that organisms could live only in the shallower and fresher portions and salts could precipitate at depth. Others believe that the Lake dried up periodically, killing off most of its plants and animal population and allowing salts to form by evaporation. Whatever its history may be, it must have almost continuously teemed with microscopic plants and animals and larger forms such as fish, turtles, alligators, pelecypods, gastropods, ostracods and others. After death, the remains of these various forms accumulated on the Lake floor in great quantities along with sand, silt, clay and other materials to produce a variety of sediments. One of the best known types is the thinly laminated "oil shale" which in reality is not a shale but a dolomitic marlstone.

Late Eocene time marks the end of the Laramide orogeny or mountain making movement. It also witnessed the final drying up or draining of Green River Lake. It was apparently a time of erosion over much of the Southern Rocky Mountains because sediments of this time are unknown and a prominent south and east sloping erosional surface can be found in many places. The only recognizable structural events were the development of the

White River uplift in late Eocene time and the uplift in the Uintas and Axial Basin anticline during most of the epoch.

During the early Tertiary, plants were essentially modern and in places were sufficiently abundant to form coals in Paleocene rocks. Living here at this time were a variety of mammals including marsupials, insectivores, rodents, tiny carnivores, and ungulates. During the Paleocene the largest of the mammals were the ungulates which reached the size of a sheep. But in the Eocene the primitive herbivore *Uintatherium* attained the bulk of a modern elephant making it the largest American land mammal of the Eocene. Appearing for the first time in the Eocene were jack rabbit-size horses, camels, rhinoceroses, elephants and even some now extinct types such as titantotheres and oreodons. Remains of birds, reptiles and fish, as well as some of the mammals listed above, have been discovered in the Wasatch Formation of the Piceance Creek basin.

Middle Tertiary [Oligocene] — The middle Tertiary probably started with a rumble, for this was the time of widespread volcanic activity in Colorado West. During the period between 40 and 25 m.y. ago, volcanic centers were most prominent in the San Juan and West Elk Mountains but there were also centers in the Rabbit Ears Range to the northeast. Thick aprons of lava flows, volcaniclastics and mudflows coalesced in the San Juan volcanic field and areas immediately to the east to form an almost continuous cover over the Southern Rockies. The result was a broad surface of subdued relief surmounted only by active volcanic edifices. The most prominent of these volcanic features were the numerous composite cones and broad collapse calderas in the San Juan field. All this volcanic activity was the surface reflection of the emplacement of two new large near-surface batholiths in the Colorado mineral belt.

In middle Tertiary time, mammals continued to increase in size. One, the rhino-like *Brontotherium* stood about eight feet high and was the largest land animal in America at this time. A few Oligocene fossils have been reported from the volcanic piles in the San Juan Mountains.

Late Tertiary [Miocene and Pliocene] —Following a period of erosion at the end of middle Tertiary time, Colorado West experienced a different brand of growing pains. The American crustal plate had continued to move westward, overriding the Eastern Pacific plate, until now it had slid over the East Pacific rise, together with its rift zone, and made contact with the Western Pacific plate. The result was a sort of crustal stretching which caused the rocks to break by extensional block faulting giving rise to outpourings of basaltic lavas. The most prominent feature produced was the Rio Grande depression, a north-south zone of block faulting lying just to the east of Colorado West and extending from Leadville on the north to the New Mexico state line and far beyond.

The outpourings of lava and cinders accompanying the faulting produced two volcanic fields; the Rio Grande field along the depression in the San Luis Valley and the North Central Colorado field centered about the Basalt area. Only the latter is in Colorado West and it consists of a number of scattered volcanic features which were probably never connected into a single lava field. Igneous rocks of late Tertiary age in this area have been divided into three categories. The first group (24 to 20 m.y. old), occur in the Flattops Primitive area, near State Bridge and north of Gypsum. The second group (14 to 9 m.y. old) are most plentiful in the Flattops Primitive Area but are also present near Steamboat Springs, just east of Glenwood Springs, at Basalt Mountain (an old shield volcano near Basalt), and as lava caps on Battlement and Grand Mesas between Rifle and Grand Junction. The third group (about 8 m.y. old) are present southeast of Glenwood Springs and possibly south of Yampa.

Uplift of some mountainous areas probably continued at a slow rate during the early part of the late Tertiary, but about 10 to 12 m.y. ago the region was subjected to major mountain building including pronounced uplift. There was reactivation of Laramide structural features, such as the Uinta Mountains, the Park and Gore Ranges, and the Uncompahgre uplift on the west side of old Uncompahgria. Large vertical faults such as those along the west side of the Gore and in the Uintas formed during the Miocene. It is estimated that there was as much as 10,000 feet of uplift in some of the ranges at this time.

Sediments of the late Tertiary are not widespread and those that are present contain much volcanic debris. Erosion of the volcanic rocks of the North Central Colorado volcanic field enabled streams to spread a belt of sediment northwestward across the Sand Wash basin and eastward into Middle Park. Some are also present in isolated areas such as those on Grand Mesa near Grand Junction.

Modern Drainage Systems—There is some evidence that present day drainage systems of Colorado West had their beginnings near the end of the Miocene Epoch, about 10 to 12 m.y. ago, probably in response to the uplift noted above and to the increased precipitation which ensued. It appears that downcutting was rapid during the Pliocene Epoch until about 8 m.y. ago and then slowed until about 1.5 m.y. ago, not long after the beginning of the Pleistocene. The period of rapid erosion probably produced the prominent entrenched meanders so common in such stream courses as the Yampa, White, Colorado, Gunnison and Dolores Rivers. It was also the time in which streams became superimposed on growing structures, such as the Dolores which crosses the Paradox salt anticline. the Yampa and Green Rivers which cross the Uinta Mountains and the Gunnison which follows the crest of the Gunnison uplift. It was also the time of the blocking of many drainages by lava flows or by uplifts, and these and other causes led to many instances of stream capture. One notable example of changes in

stream drainage is that of the Gunnison River near its mouth. Prior to the Miocene uplift it probably flowed westward across the Uncompahgre uplift via Unaweep Canyon to join the Dolores River near Gateway. When the Uncompahgre began to rise in Pliocene time, the River was unable to cut its valley into the Precambrian core rapidly enough to keep pace, and it soon spilled over into or was captured by a tributary of the Colorado River. Its abandoned course was later modified by tongues of ice in the Pleistocene.

Quaternary Events—The volcanic activity, which had produced the North Central Colorado volcanic field during the Miocene and Pliocene, continued at a much reduced rate during the Pleistocene and Holocene Epochs. Volcanic rocks with ages of less than 1.5 m.y. can be seen as flows and small cones about nine miles northwest of Aspen, just northeast of McCoy and at Dotsero, the latter being the youngest (about 4,000 years old).

Erosion has been relatively rapid in Colorado West since early Pleistocene (1.5 to 3 m.y. ago). This accelerated rate has been due largely to four or five periods of greatly increased rainfall (pluvial periods) directly related to melting of the great continental ice sheets which covered the northern part of our continent at least four times (Nebraskan, Kansan, Illinoisian and Wisconsin Ice Ages) during the Pleistocene. It is conceivable that as much as 300 to 500 inches of precipitation per year fell on Colorado West mountains and valleys during each rainy period, as compared to the present rates of 8 to 40 inches per year. Much of this moisture came from the melting of the continental ice sheets, but much also was derived from melting of ice in the mountains of Colorado West. There is growing evidence that nearly all the higher portions of this part of Colorado were crowned by ice caps during some or all of the glacial ages. These caps most likely covered much of the high mountains and even somewhat lower areas such as the White River Plateau,

Grand Mesa, Uncompahgre Plateau and the Roan Plateau. Many of the higher areas of Colorado West bear witness to these multiple glaciations. For example, the San Juan Mountains show evidence of having been scoured by valley ice once during the Illinoisian and at least twice during the Wisconsin. Grand Mesa bears the scars of at least two Wisconsin ice caps and their outlet tongues, the latter ploughing down the Mesa sides to elevations as low as 5,400 feet above sea level. Unaweep Canyon, the abandoned canyon described above, was modified by ice masses spilling into the Canyon from ice caps on the Uncompahgre crest at least two times during the Pleistocene. Moraines (heaps of glacial debris) occur at both ends of the Canyon; those at the west end being at an elevation of less than 5,600 feet. These moraines have been tentatively dated as Nebraskan and Kansan. Small cirques (bowl-shaped excavations) on the Canyon sides are of Wisconsin age.

The prolonged periods of rainfall following each glaciation caused rapid erosion of cliffs and broadening and deepening of valleys. Rock detritus worn from high cliffs was spread out into valleys to produce broad gravel aprons or bajadas, whose nearly flat upper surfaces (bajada plains) are sometimes referred to as pediments. These bajadas coalesced in stream valleys with outwash gravels deposited by swollen streams draining from melting ice caps and valley glaciers. Downcutting during interglacial times removed much of the outwash deposits leaving the remnants as terraces above the new stream level. In places five or more terrace and bajada remnants may be visible along the sides of a valley.

We know very little about local plant and animal life during the Pleistocene but bog samples from Grand Mesa indicate an abundance of conifers. The lower valleys must have been untenable during the meltwater or pluvial phases but at other times there were undoubtedly forests and grasslands in which mammoths, mastodons, rhinos and other ice age animals thrived. Most of the evidence for such conclusions has long since vanished, but teeth of the wooly mammoth have been found in outwash gravels near Grand Junction and Montrose.

CARVING UP THE AREA
[Major Geologic Subdivisions of Colorado West]

As noted previously, Colorado West has a wide variety of topographic regions ranging from nearly flat featureless lowlands to areas of buttes and broad mesas, to regions of high plateaus and deep canyons, and finally to clusters of lofty and extremely rugged mountains. Most of these regions owe their basic features to the titanic forces of orogeny which wrinkled and split the crust of the Earth and spewed out great volumes of molten rock during the orogenic events described previously. The final touches have since been applied by wind, running water, glacial ice, gravity and even by organisms such as man.

Sags in the Crust [Large Downwarps]:
In Colorado West there are four greatly downwarped segments of the crust which are referred to as structural basins. Even though these regions are depressed, they do not appear as topographic lows on the surface. Instead, they are generally filled with rocks younger than those preserved in the surrounding uplifts, and may actually stand higher than bordering areas. Downwarps discussed here are Piceance Creek, Sand Wash, Paradox and San Juan basins.

Piceance Creek Basin:—One of the major structural features of Colorado West is the Piceance Creek basin. It is an elongate northwest-southeast trending downwarp covering an area of approximately 9,000 square miles in the northwest portion of Colorado (this includes such transitional areas as the Carbonera sag, Junction bench and Montrose sag. Lying entirely in the Colorado Plateau province, it is bordered on the north by the Axial fold belt, on the east by the White River uplift (including the Grand Hogback) and Elk Mountains, on the south by the West Elk Mountains, on the southwest by the Uncompahgre Plateau and on the west by the Douglas Creek arch.

This area probably first became a basin during the Laramide orogeny about 70 m.y. ago. At that time it started to subside and soon began to receive sediments eroded from the higher surrounding areas, much of it from the Park Range to the southeast. The down-folded rocks included Precambrian

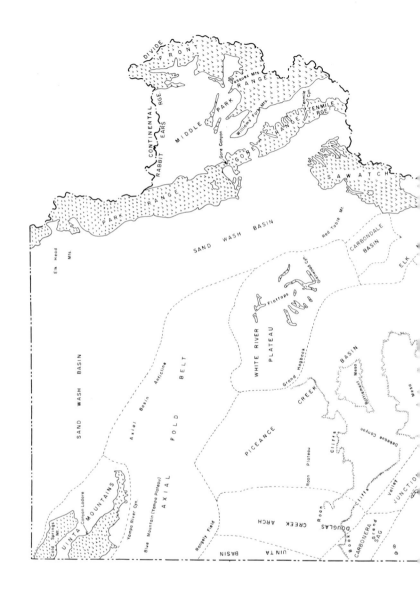

Fig. 5–Major geologic subdivisions

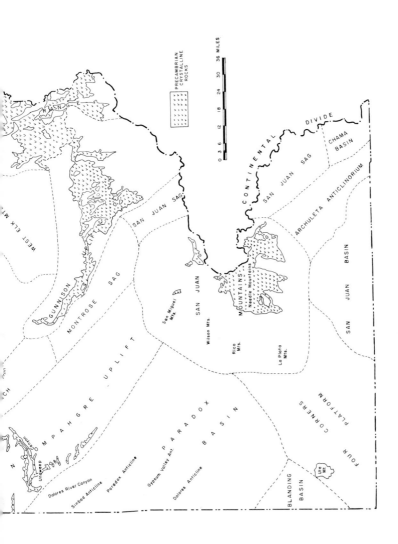

PRECAMBRIAN
CRYSTALLINE
ROCKS

0 6 12 18 24 30 36 MILES

RANGE

WEST ELK MT

GUNNISON UPLIFT

MONTROSE SAG

SAN JUAN SAG

CONTINENTAL DIVIDE

CHAMA BASIN

ARCHULETA ANTICLINORIUM

SAN JUAN SAG

MOUNTAINS
Needle Mountains

SAN JUAN

San Miguel Mts.

Wilson Mts.

Rico Mts.

La Plata Mts.

SAN JUAN BASIN

PAHGRE UPLIFT

Unaweep Canyon

Dolores River Canyon

Sinbad Anticline

Paradox Anticline

Gypsum Valley Ant.

Dolores Anticline

PARADOX BASIN

FOUR CORNERS PLATFORM

BLANDING BASIN

Ute Mt.

45

basement rocks and overlying Paleozoic and Mesozoic strata totaling as much as 18,000 feet in the deeper portion of the basin near its northeastern margin. As much as 9,000 feet of Tertiary stream and lake deposits accumulated in the subsiding basin; consequently, it is considered to be 27,000 feet deep. Subsidence ceased during the Eocene, the lake which occupied it was drained, and deposition was essentially halted. Regional uplift elevated the Basin in late Tertiary time and initiated the erosion which has prevailed since.

Although this region is primarily a structural basin, uplift and erosion along its borders have created some spectacular features. Some of the more important ones are as follows:

1]. *Grand Mesa*-Just east of Grand Junction stands Grand Mesa, a broad flat topped erosional remnant rising to an elevation of 11,234 feet at its highest point, Leon Peak. The summit area of the Mesa is about 800 square miles, it averages about 10,000 feet in elevation and towers about 6,000 feet above the adjacent valleys of the Gunnison and Colorado Rivers. Exposed rocks are gently dipping Cretaceous and Tertiary sediments capped by as much as 400 feet of basaltic lava flows. One flow has been dated at 9.7 m.y. ago (early Pliocene). The lava forms a "Y"-shaped outcrop pattern with the tail to the east suggesting that it filled an old stream system draining in that direction. The source of the lava appears to have been large fissures a few miles to the east and implies that lava must have flowed westward up the old drainage channels. Since its formation, erosion has carved away the former valley sides and left the old lava-fill standing high above the surrounding terrain.

In the Pleistocene, the Mesa top was host to two or more thick ice caps which spread over most of the upland surface and, in places, cascaded downward along old stream courses on the Mesa flanks. During and following the ice ages, large slumps on the margins of the Mesa produced a broad "landslide" bench of rotated lava blocks behind which formed many small lakes. In all, there are some 300 lakes on the bench and top of Grand Mesa. Most of them are stocked with game fish making this an anglers' paradise.

Figure 6—Aerial view of Grand Mesa. Lava flows cap snow-blanketed Tertiary rocks. Cretaceous strata form lower two thirds.

2.] *Battlement Mesa*-About 15 miles north of Grand Mesa and just south of the town of Rifle is a similar but smaller lava-capped mesa, referred to as Battlement Mesa. It has a surface area of only about 20 square miles but is some 20 miles long and reaches an elevation of 11,165 feet at North Mamm Peak. The lava is confined to the east end of the Mesa and to a possible outlier on Mt. Callahan across the Colorado River from the Mesa.

The history of Battlement Mesa is similar to that of Grand Mesa. The lava cap is of probable Pliocene age, and appears to have been formed by flows filling an east to southeast trending valley. Cirque-like excavations on both north and south flanks suggest modification by glacial ice during the Pleistocene.

3.] *Roan Plateau*-A prominent feature near the southern edge of the Piceance Creek basin is the Roan Plateau, a high region of relatively uniform elevation formed by outcrops of resistant sediments dipping gently northward toward the deeper portion of the Basin. The Plateau is about 70 miles long, extending from near the Utah state line to near Rifle, and

Figure 7—Book Cliffs escarpment near Palisade. Lower slope made by Mancos Shale. Steep cliffs and overlying rocks are Mesaverde Group.

averages about 30 miles wide. It is partly dissected by numerous northward flowing tributaries of Piceance Creek and some southward flowing streams draining into the Colorado River. Elevations at the crest average about 8,000 feet, but some points exceed 9,000 feet.

Because of its elevation and broad upland surface, the Roan Plateau probably was covered by ice caps and supported small valley glaciers one or more times during the Pleistocene. Since then the higher portions of the Plateau have become covered with grasslands and juniper-pinyon forests which serve as wintering grounds for the world's largest herd of mule deer, estimated to number in the neighborhood of 60,000 head.

In addition to its broad and lofty configuration, the Plateau has two other striking topographic features. Along its southern edge it is terminated by two towering cliffs or erosional escarpments, one above the other. The lowermost is the Book Cliffs, a prominent cliff of resistant Cretaceous Mesaverde sandstones and coal-bearing rocks rising 1,500 to 2,000 feet above the broad Grand Valley carved into the weak Mancos shale by the Colorado River. The Cliffs extend from Palisade westward to the Utah state line and continue from there another 180 miles into central Utah. Prominent coals of the Book Cliffs coal field can be seen in the Cliffs in many localities.

Above the Book Cliffs and some 5 to 12 miles farther north are the Roan Cliffs, formed by resistant sandy and marly beds of the Eocene Green River and Uinta Formations. The Roan Cliffs can be traced for about 80 miles from Rifle west to the Utah state line. In most places the steep upper portion of these Cliffs is formed by high-grade "oil shale", the richest zone of which is the "Mahogany Ledge". This rich zone (up to 50 gallons of oil per ton) may be only 30 to 40 feet thick where exposed in the Cliffs but thickens to more than 1,000 feet in the center of the Basin some 20 miles or so to the north.

Another interesting aspect of the Piceance Creek basin is that it contains much of Colorado West's petroleum reserves. Thousands of test holes have been drilled here, primarily on the shallow flanks of the Basin. As a result, oil and natural gas have been discovered in at least a dozen different geologic units ranging in age from Pennsylvanian to Tertiary.

An additional resource of this Basin is its coal. Late Cretaceous rocks, which are present throughout most of the Basin, contain an estimated 60 billion tons of bituminous coal.

The Basin is also noted for its unusual fossils. Paleozoic rocks are not exposed, hence we know little about their fossil content. Mesozoic rocks, however, are more widespread and some units are fossiliferous. One of these is the Morrison Formation of Late Jurassic age. Along the southern margin of the Basin, where it

Figure 8—Mt. Logan near De Beque. Roan Cliffs here are formed by light colored Green River Formation capped by rounded knobs of Uinta Formation. Steep cliff near top is made by Mahogany Ledge. Red beds near base are Wasatch Formation.

begins to rise onto the Uncompahgre Plateau, the unit is well exposed and has yielded the remains of numerous dinosaurs. The remarkable thing about these dinosaur bones is that they include those of the three largest ever discovered in the world. The largest is the so-called "Supersaurus", represented by a scapula (shoulder blade) some eight feet long, together with other bones, discovered in 1972 on Dry Mesa in Mesa County. The second largest is represented by a humerus (leg bone) some seven feet long from Winter Mesa in Delta County and the third is a partial skeleton, including a humerus measuring six feet eight inches long, from Riggs Hill near Grand Junction. All three of these giants appear to belong to the genus *Brachiosaurus*, a plant eating sauropod reptile. "Supersaurus" had a 50 foot long neck enabling him to stand some 70 feet high at the shoulders and weigh in at about 80 tons. Numerous other remains have been found in the Morrison including those of carnivorous dinosaurs (carnosaurs), crocodiles, turtles, flying reptiles (pterosaurs), mammals, pelecypods, gastropods and several varieties of plants.

The overlying Cretaceous Dakota Group contains large quantities of dinosaur "gizzard stones", pelecypods, gastropods, cephalopods and numerous plant remains. The Cretaceous Mancos shale contains an invertebrate fauna of pelecypods, gastropods, cephalopods, and microscopic foraminifera. The Cretaceous Mesaverde Group contains some pelecypods, gastropods and abundant plant remains. The Paleocene and Eocene Wasatch Formation has yielded the remains of early mammals as well as those of turtles, fish and birds. The thinly layered units of the Eocene Green River Formation are noted for excellently preserved fish, turtle and alligator skeletons as well as bird tracks and impressions of feathers, leaves, larvae, and many winged insects.

Sand Wash Basin:—The Sand Wash basin, in northernmost Colorado West, is an east-west elongated structural depression representing an extension of the Wyoming Basin Province. It is comprised of some 4,000 square miles bounded on the north by Cherokee Ridge arch at the Wyoming state line, on the south and west by the Uinta arch and Axial fold belt, and on the east by the Park Range. A southward projecting tongue separates the Park

Figure 9—De Beque Canyon of Colorado River. The river here is deeply incised where it crosses the Roan and Book Cliffs area.

Range from the Sawatch-Uinta trend. The Basin is sometimes considered as a southern extension of the Washakie basin of southern Wyoming.

Topographically the Basin is quite irregular, consisting of a rough, deeply dissected surface formed on Cretaceous and Tertiary sediments. The higher areas are generally supported by uplifted older rocks and Tertiary intrusions. Elevations range from about 5,000 feet near the confluence of the Little Snake and Yampa Rivers to more than 11,000 feet in the Elk Head Mountains.

The Sand Wash basin became a structural basin in Late Cretaceous or early Tertiary time. The Precambrian basement together with the overlying 17,000 feet of Mesozoic and Paleozoic sediments subsided sufficiently to accommodate the accumulation of about 9,000 feet of Cenozoic stream, wind and lake deposits. At present the basement lies at 17,500 feet below sea level in the center of the Basin. Structural relief between this Basin and the adjacent Uinta Mountains uplift (9,000 feet above sea level) is about 26,500 feet.

Perhaps the most scenic area in the Basin is that of the Elk Head Mountains, a volcanic pile reaching an elevation of more than 11,000 feet at the eastern edge of the structure.

Economic deposits include numerous extensive bituminous coal beds seen in exposures of the Cretaceous Mesaverde Group between Craig and Oak Creek. It is estimated that the coal reserves in this Basin total some 58 billion tons. There also has been considerable production of oil and gas from Tertiary formations in the Basin, and a Miocene unit (Browns Park Formation) has yielded uranium from open pit mines near Maybell.

Paradox Basin:—One of the most geologically unusual portions of Colorado West is that 4,500 square mile portion of the Paradox basin which extends into the State from Utah. It is a much dissected area of mesas and canyons bounded on the northeast by the Uncompahgre uplift and on the south by the Four Corners platform. Elevations in the Basin range from about 4,500 feet near Gateway to more than 8,600 feet north of Sinbad Valley on the east flank of the La Sal Mountains, just across the border in Utah.

Fig 10—Volcanic plug near Toponas

During the early Paleozoic this area was a broad shelf on which there accumulated a thin cover of sandstone, shale and limestone, but in the Pennsylvanian it was downfaulted and downwarped into a deep northwest trending trough. In this trough was deposited as much as 10,000 feet of arkose, black shale, limestone, gypsum, salt and other evaporites. Subsequent burial by 10,000 or more feet of Mesozoic and Cenozoic rocks produced differential loading and caused the thousands of feet of salt to become mobile. The result was the formation of four prominent northwest trending anticlines with intrusive cores of salt. Subsequent erosion stripped most of the Cenozoic and Mesozoic cover from the folds and allowed water to penetrate into the cores. These waters removed much of the salt in the upper parts of the folds and allowed the overlying rocks to collapse.

Outstanding features of this area include the Dolores, Gypsum Valley, Paradox and Sinbad salt anticlines. As noted above, the centers have collapsed on most of these anticlines due to solution of the salt, and the result has been the formation of broad valleys such as Paradox Valley and Gypsum

Valley. The Dolores River, one of the northward flowing rivers in this area, follows the crest of the Dolores anticline for many miles before cutting directly across the Gypsum Valley and Paradox anticlines; hence the name "Paradox". It has been suggested that either the River formed in flat-lying sediments and carved its way downward into the folded rocks or it was there when the folding began and managed to cut through the rocks as they were folded.

Another spectacular feature of this area is the canyon of the Dolores River from Paradox Valley to Gateway. Throughout much of this distance the stream flows in a narrow meandering red-hued canyon bordered by vertical cliffs of Triassic Wingate Sandstone and lesser cliffs and slopes of other variegated Triassic and Jurassic units. A flume constructed in the 1890's to carry water to gold placer deposits above the River can be seen below the junction with the San Miguel River near Uravan.

Most of the uranium and vanadium produced in Colorado has come from this area, the bulk of it from an arcuate belt referred to as the Uravan mineral belt. Some eight to ten million tons of ore containing 40 to 50 million pounds of uranium oxide and 160 to 200 million pounds of vanadium oxide have been mined

Figure 11—Elk River near Steamboat Springs

from ore bodies in paleostream deposits of the Jurassic Morrison Formation in this area since mining began near the turn of the century. Several mills and innumerable mines have operated in the area during the exploitation of its uranium-vanadium deposits.

San Juan Basin:—The San Juan basin is a structural feature which lies mostly in New Mexico but a small portion, about 900 square miles, projects into Colorado just south of the San Juan Mountains. It is bounded on the north and northeast by the San Juan Mountains and on the west by the Four Corners platform. This segment of the Basin has been dissected by stream erosion to produce a terrain consisting largely of broad pinyon covered mesas and deep youthful valleys. Elevations range from a low of about 4,700 feet, where the Mancos River enters New Mexico, to a high of 8,824 feet at Menefee Peak near the town of Mancos.

During the Paleozoic and Mesozoic Eras this area was subjected to a variety of structural, erosional and depositional processes which resulted in the accumulation of 10,000 to 12,000 feet of sediment. The Basin formed primarily during the Laramide orogeny with the greatest downwarping occurring near the Colorado-New Mexico line. This deep, which is now about 6,900 feet below sea level, coincides with a late Paleozoic trough along the southwest side of the ancient Uncompahgre highland. As much as 5,000 feet of Cenozoic sediments accumulated in the depression formed by the Laramide downwarping.

Economic products of the Basin are primarily oil and natural gas, produced mostly from rocks of Cretaceous age. The Cretaceous is also important for its contained reserves of bituminous coal. It is estimated that this portion of the Basin contains as much as 27 billion tons of the black stuff.

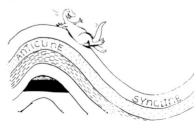

Some Big Wrinkles:

As noted previously, when mountain building began during the Laramide orogeny, some portions of Colorado West were downwarped, some were upwarped and still other remained essentially un-deformed. Here we are concerned with the large un-warped areas which, though some may reach elevations in excess of 10,000 feet, do not form spectacular mountains in Colorado West. Nevertheless, most are large and generally prominent features which owe much of their present relief to late Cenozoic uplift.

Uinta Mountains:—At the extreme northwest corner of Colorado West is the eastern end of the Uinta Mountains, a huge east-west trending of anticlinal arch confined largely to Utah but ex-tending some 35 miles into Colorado. The nor-thern portion of the mountain is commonly called Cold Springs Mountain. Elevations in this area range from about 6,400 feet near the confluence of the Green and Yampa Riv-ers to 9,006 feet at Zenobia Park in the Uintas.

The Uinta Mountains are an elongate asym-metrical feature about 35 miles wide bordered on the north side by a major Laramide re-verse fault (Uinta fault) and on the south side by

Figure 12—Steamboat Rock on Yampa River in Dinosaur National Monument. Monolith formed by Navajo (Nugget) Sandstone.

56

smaller faults and subsidiary folds. This eastern end, which is split by an axial graben of Laramide age, plunges southeastward to join the somewhat lower arcuate trend of the Axial Basin anticline. Both features are part of an essentially continuous fold system or trend which begins with the Uintas, drops somewhat into the Axial Basin anticline, rises in the White River uplift, drops into a saddle near the Colorado River, rises again in the Elk Mountains and continues southward the length of the Sawatch Range.

During the Paleozoic and Mesozoic as much as 17,000 feet of sediment accumulated upon the basement rocks in this area, but in early Laramide time the fold began to rise and the crest was stripped of its Paleozoic and Mesozoic cover. Other periods of uplift occurred in the Eocene and the Oligocene and in the early Miocene an east trending paleovalley was cut along the crest of the Uinta arch. The valley was filled with erosional debris in the late Miocene, just prior to the collapse of this end of the arch and the formation of the large graben noted above. It was during this last phase that the Green and Yampa Rivers became incised in their courses across the fold.

The most spectacular scenic areas of this region are Yampa River Canyon and Canyon Ladore of the Green River, both of which are included in Dinosaur National Monument.

Axial Fold Belt:—As noted above, the high standing Uinta anticline is connected with the equally high White River uplift by a relatively low arch referred to as the Axial Basin anticline or uplift. This somewhat arcuate uplift, consisting of a number of subsidiary anticlines and synclines, is about 45 miles long and ten miles wide and comprises the northern portion of the Axial fold belt. The northeast side of the uplift is marked by an abrupt transition into the Sand Wash basin along a belt of steeply inclined and faulted Cretaceous and Tertiary beds. The southwestern portion of the fold belt consists of a number of large anticlines and intervening synclines. Some of the better known are Blue Mountain, Rangely, Skull Creek, Cross Mountain, Danforth Hills, Maudlin Gulch and Wilson Creek anticlines.

This has never been a very high region since its beginning in the Paleocene, but it served to separate the Green River basin

Figure 13—Blue Mountain near Dinosaur

into two parts in Eocene time. It was reactivated in the late Tertiary, and since then the Tertiary rocks have been largely removed. Present elevations along this trend vary from about 5,970 feet along the Yampa River at the west end to 7,920 feet on Juniper Mountain near the middle and to 8,720 feet on the Danforth Hills at the eastern end.

Economically this is a very important part of Colorado West. Although its population is sparse, it is rich in natural resources. Many of the anticlines such as Rangely, Danforth Hills, Maudlin Gulch, Wilson Creek, Thornburg, Iles, Juniper Mountain and Elk Springs have produced large amounts of oil and natural gas from Paleozoic and Mesozoic rocks.

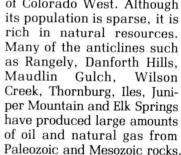

58

Multiple coal beds (12 or more in some places) occur in the Upper Cretaceous Mesaverde Group throughout much of the uplift.

White River Uplift:—The White River uplift is a domal upwarp still largely covered by a blanket of Paleozoic sediments. Volcanic rocks of late Cenozoic age crown the northeast part of the uplift to create the Flattops, the highest area of the White River Plateau. The uplift measures about 50 miles in an east-west direction and 40 miles north-south. It is bounded on the north by a series of lesser folds including those of the Axial Basin anticline. Bordering it on the east is the Eagle River basin, a southeastward projecting tongue of the Sand Wash basin, and on the west is the Piceance Creek basin. Dips on the east and north sides are relatively gentle; but on the west and southwest sides, along the Grand Hogback, the beds approach the vertical and in some places are somewhat overturned. Westward thrusting has been reported at depth along the hogback, and large normal faults are common along the south flank near Glenwood Springs.

Figure 14—Grand Hogback near Rifle. Tertiary and Cretaceous strata here stand nearly vertical and resistant sandstones form flatirons.

This area was relatively stable during Paleozoic and Mesozoic time and was covered by 15,000 or more feet of sediment. There is evidence of slight movement in the Paleocene but major uplift began in early middle Eocene time to produce the last of the Laramide mountains in Colorado West. Three periods of volcanic activity followed the uplift; the first about 24 to 20 m.y. ago, the second about 14 to 10 m.y. ago and the third approximately 7.5 m.y. ago. The result was the production of a large high region ranging in elevation from about 6,600 feet on the south flank to 12, 493 feet at Flattop Mountain near the north end.

The most attractive features of the White River uplift are Glenwood Canyon and the Glenwood hot springs on the south end, Grand Hogback on the western side, and Trappers Lake and the Flattops Wilderness Area in the northeastern uplands.

There have been very few attempts to exploit minerals of the Uplift. Some uranium-vanadium deposits have been mined at Uranium Peak west of Meeker and on East Rifle Creek north of Rifle, and limestone has been quarried at Glenwood Springs.

Figure 15—Glenwood Canyon at south end of White River Uplift. Rock layers here are Cambrian quartzite and Ordovician dolomite.

Figure 16—Folded Paleozoic strata in Sweetwater Canyon near Dotsero.

Uncompahgre Uplift:—Extending northwestward for some 100 miles from the San Juan Mountains into eastern Utah and serving as the southwestern flank of the Uinta basin, is the prominent Uncompahgre uplift. This 25 to 30 mile wide anticlinal structure is actually a remnant of old Uncompahgria, that late Paleozoic mountain range which covered much of Colorado West. The western border of the old mountain mass was reactivated in Late Jurassic time, again in Laramide time and finally reached its present elevation in the late Cenozoic. The uplift occurred mainly along faults on both flanks. In places these faults have broken through the overlying rocks, such as does the Redlands fault near Grand Junction, but in most places the rocks were warped and stretched to form steep monoclines over the faulted rocks at depth.

Erosion did not keep pace with uplift but did manage to strip off the thousands of feet of Tertiary and Late Cretaceous rocks which once covered it. In most places resistant sandstones of the Dakota Group retarded the downcutting, and as a result much of the Plateau now consists of Dakota rocks capping a thin

Figure 17—Unaweep Canyon bisecting Uncompahgre uplift. This part of former valley of Gunnison River shows U-shape characteristic of glaciated valleys.

section of Jurassic and Triassic rocks which, in turn, rest unconformably on Precambrian rocks. Some streams on the flanks have cut through the sediments and into the Precambrian rocks.

Topographically, the Uncompahgre presents an almost featureless surface. Numerous small canyons have been carved into the flanks, but two of them—Unaweep Canyon and Ruby Canyon of the Colorado River—cross the axis of the uplift. Elevations increase southward from a low of about 4,300 feet in Ruby Canyon at the north end to 10,338 feet on Horsefly Peak near the south end.

One of the major attractions of the Uncompahgre is Unaweep Canyon which crosses the Plateau about 15 airline miles southwest of Grand Junction. Unaweep is a Ute Indian word meaning "canyon with two mouths." It is a broad U-shaped canyon which averages 3,000 feet in depth, ranges from one-fourth mile to a mile in width and trends across the axis of the uplift for a distance of about 22 miles. Instead of containing a large stream, it now is occupied only by small underfit streams draining in either direction from a low divide on the valley floor at an elevation of 7,200 feet. West Creek wanders westward for

Figure 18—Colorado National Monument at north end of Uncompahgre uplift. Massive Wingate Sandstone capped by thin layer of Keyenta Formation forms steep cliffs and monoliths such as Independence Monument shown here.

16 miles before entering a narrow canyon and continuing to its confluence with the Dolores River near Gateway. East Creek drains the eastern six miles of Unaweep Canyon before entering a narrower canyon and eventually entering the Gunnison River near Whitewater. It is believed that the Canyon was cut by a river, probably the Gunnison, during the Pliocene. Uplift near the end of that epoch caused the stream to abandon it. Ice caps covered the Plateau at various times in the Pleistocene and during the Nebraskan and Kansan stages ice spilled into the Canyon, filling it nearly to the brim and causing ice tongues to move away from the divide in both directions as outlet glaciers. As the ice moved, it widened and smoothed out the Canyon. The ice tongues stopped at the points where the canyons now narrow; hence Unaweep Canyon, the wide glaciated portion of the old valley, now contrasts sharply with the narrow unglaciated lower parts of West and East Creek. After the ice tongues melted, small cirque glaciers gouged into the valley walls in places leaving amphitheatre-like reentrants. Later rock falls have added to the valley fill, concealing much of the glacial debris.

Another attractive portion is Colorado National Monument, a 30-square-mile area along the steep northeast margin of the uplift just west of Grand Junction. In this area streams and probably glacial ice have carved deep canyons into the flank of the structure creating spectacular cliffs of Triassic Wingate and Jurassic Entrada Sandstones.

Economic contributions of the Plateau include uranium-vanadium deposits on Outlaw, Calamity and Tenderfoot Mesas as well as minor amounts of beryl, fluorospar, quartz and copper.

Douglas Creek Arch:—Extending north from near the north end of the Uncompahgre uplift is Douglas Creek arch, a low upwarp some 10 miles wide and 50 miles long which separates the Piceance Creek basin from the Uinta basin to the west. The Arch is characterized by a series of *en echelon* northwest trending subsidiary anticlines that are subparallel to the Uncompahgre uplift to the south and Rangely anticline to the north. On top of the Precambrian the Arch appears as a north-plunging anticlinal nose.

The history of the Arch is relatively simple. It began as a low upwarp in Late Jurassic time. Cretaceous and Tertiary sediments thin significantly across the structure indicating intermittent growth during those periods. The structure has never stood very high; consequently, its cover is mostly dissected Tertiary and Cretaceous rocks. Elevations range from a low of about 6,000 feet at the north end to a high of 9,090 feet near Douglas Pass not far from the south end.

Economic products of the Arch include large volumes of natural gas as well as minor amounts of oil and bituminous coal.

Gunnison Uplift:—Projecting into the south end of the Piceance Creek basin is a northwest plunging asymmetric anticline some 65 miles long and up to 20 miles wide. The northern flank merges into the north-sloping southern flank of the Piceance Creek basin but the southern side is bounded for most of its length by a large normal fault.

The Gunnison uplift, like the Uncompahgre uplift, is a part of the old Uncompahgre highland of the late Paleozoic. The mountains wore down slowly and the Gunnison uplift area was finally covered by encroaching sediments in the Late Jurassic. As much as 12,000 feet of Mesozoic and Cenozoic sediments accumulated here before uplift began, probably in late Miocene or early Pliocene time. As the fold began to rise, its crest was breached by erosion and the ancestral Gunnison River began to entrench itself along the fold axis. Since that time the River has carved a vertical-walled gorge nearly 2,000 feet deep into dark colored Precambrian gneisses in the core of the uplift. This gorge, referred to as the Black Canyon of the Gunnison, lies almost entirely within the Black Canyon of the Gunnison National Monument. The Canyon has been dammed at various points to store water for power generation and for recreational purposes. The uppermost of these has created Blue Mesa Reservoir, a 20-mile-long haven for anglers and boaters.

Small amounts of gypsum, quartz, feldspar and copper have been mined from the western half of the uplift and somewhat larger deposits of uranium, copper, lead, gold and silver have been extracted from various localities along the eastern half.

High and Lofty Places:
To many visitors and natives the most breath-taking and appealing real-estate in Colorado West is that of the majestic

Figure 19—Black Canyon of the Gunnison National Monument. River flows in deep gorge cut into Precambrian Black Canyon Schist.

Figure 20—Crest of Sawatch Range near Independence Pass. Glaciated valley leads down from glacial cirque (bowl) in distance.

mountain ranges. Some of these towering rock masses are the result of outpourings of volcanic materials (San Juan and West Elk Mountains), but others are the result of erosion of huge anticlinal arches (Uinta, Park, Gore and Sawatch Ranges.) Each of these is described briefly herein.

Sawatch Range:—The Sawatch Range is the Precambrian core of a broad anticlinal arch trending generally northward from the east end of the Gunnison uplift and occupying the site of the late Paleozoic Central Colorado trough. It is about 85 miles long and as much as 35 miles wide. The west side of the Range is bordered by steeply inclined faults and by reverse faults dipping into the Range. The west flank is further complicated by the development, within the arch, of a synclinal valley now occupied by the Roaring Fork River. West of this syncline lie the Elk Mountains, a subsidiary fold range to be described later. The main axis of the Sawatch Range plunges gradually northward into a saddle near the Colorado River.

During the early Paleozoic, the old Precambrian gneiss, schist and granite of this area were gradually covered by a thin sequence of sandstone, shale and limestone. In the late

Paleozoic, however, this portion of Colorado West subsided to form a deep trough in which more than 10,000 feet of arkose, sandstone, shale, limestone, gypsum and salt accumulated. Following a long interval of erosion, a thin layer of Jurassic sediments covered the area, only to be followed by many thousands of feet of Cretaceous deposits. The fold began to rise about 70 m.y. ago in early Laramide times and continued to rise for the next 3 m.y. Between 72 and 60 m.y. ago, thousands of stocks, dikes and sills were intruded into the structure. The earliest of these occur on the flanks and give evidence of being later than the uplift and the flank faults. By Paleocene time most of the sediments had been removed from the crest, and by late Paleocene time extensive volcanic activity had occurred. Much of the present elevation of the Range is probably due to late Cenozoic uplift.

Water and ice have ravaged the crest since the last uplift so that today the high parts of the Range are craggy areas of nearly bare rock extending well above timberline. It includes 10 peaks over 14,000 feet in elevation, among which are Mt. Elbert (14,433), Mt. Massive (14,421) and Mt. Harvard (14,420). Mt. Elbert, Colorado's highest mountain, lies just east of the continental divide and cannot be claimed by Colorado West.

This Range has long been exploited for its mineral riches. Beginning in the late 1880's prospectors made numerous discoveries of gold, silver, lead, zinc, iron and other metals. Many deposits were commercial and led to the establishment of such famous mining districts as Monarch, Tomichi, Gold Brick-Pitkin, Chalk Creek, Tincup, Spring Creek, Ruby-Elk Mountain, Lincoln Gulch, Aspen, Sugar Loaf-St. Kevin, Fulford, Gilman, Red Cliff and many lesser ones. In more recent times uranium has been discovered and mined at Marshall Pass and limestone has been quarried at Garfield.

Major attractions in the Range are its many high peaks, the numerous ghost towns and its excellent ski facilities. The ski slopes of the Vail area adorn the north plunging nose of the anticline, but other ski resorts are located at such places as Monarch Pass, Crested Butte and Copper Mountain.

Figure 21—Maroon Bells in Elk Mountains near Aspen. Mountains are composed of rocks of Maroon Formation of Pennsylvanian and Permian age.

Elk Mountains:—As noted earlier, a subsidiary fold on the flank of the Sawatch Range has been eroded to form the northwest-trending Elk Mountains, some 30 miles long and 15 miles wide. The west flank of the Elk Mountains, bordering the Piceance Creek basin, is monoclinal (a continuation of the Grand Hogback) but is complicated by faulting and northwest-plunging *en echelon* folds.

The Elk Mountains area was within the Central Colorado trough and has an early history similar to that of the Sawatch Range area. Not long after the Sawatch Range began to rise in early Laramide time, the Elk Mountains anticline formed on its west flank. As the Sawatch continued to rise during the Paleocene, the subsidiary anticline moved downslope by gliding to form the Elk Mountain thrust. The Paleozoic and Mesozoic strata of this subsidiary fold were extensively intruded by igneous rocks in Oligocene time, 34 to 29 m.y. ago. Some of these intrusives may have reached the surface to form volcanoes but no volcanic rocks are preserved.

There must have been pronounced vertical uplift in this area during the late Cenozoic, followed by considerable stream erosion and several stages of Pleistocene glaciation. The resulting topography is nothing short of spectacular. Folded and faulted sediments have been dissected by water and ice to produce deep valleys and high jagged peaks with vertical cliffs of brightly colored Paleozoic sediments and some dull colored intrusives. Six peaks in these mountains are higher than 14,000 feet, with the highest being Maroon Peak (14,156feet).

Treasure Mountain, North Pole Basin, Sheep Mountain and Lead King Basin have yielded a moderate amount of lead, zinc, silver, gold and copper. In addition, beautiful snow white Yule Marble was quarried for many years on Yule Creek three miles southeast of Marble. It was used in many structures including the Lincoln Memorial and the Tomb of the Unknown Soldier.

Major scenic attractions in the Elk Mountains include: 1) Maroon Bells, a series of high peaks with vertical cliffs of red sandstone and shale towering above verdant valleys sculptured by ice; 2). Crystal River valley, a crystal clear stream which, with the aid of glacial ice, has cut a deep gorge into the west side of the mountains, and 3). the numerous Aspen ski courses constructed on the northeast flank of the mountains.

Park Range: —Forming the western side of North and Middle Parks is a long north-south ridge extending from the Wyoming border to near the town of McCoy, a distance of about 75 miles. The northern part of this ridge, marking the western edge of the higher mountains of the State, is called the Park Range. It is generally anticlinal in structure, in the northern part; but in the southern part, faults on the western margin modify the simple pattern.

The area covered by this Range lay along the western edge of old Frontrangia in late Paleozoic times, thus it received no sediments until the Jurassic. It was later covered by less than 10,000 feet of Cretaceous rocks. Uplift of the Range began in latest Cretaceous time and the thin cover of sediments was soon stripped off exposing the old Precambrian core. After a long period of erosion there was renewed uplift and flank faulting in late Cenozoic time. Stream and glacial erosion since the last uplift have produced extensive exposures of Precambrian basement rock. Numerous portions of the Range stand above

Figure 22—Hahns Peak north of Steamboat Springs

11,000 feet, but the highest peaks are Mt. Zirkel (12,180 feet) and Flattop Mountain (12,118 feet).

Mineral deposits are not common in the Park Range, but gold has been mined at Hahns Peak, north of Steamboat Springs. Scenic attractions include the mineral and hot springs at Steamboat Springs and the Mt. Werner ski area east of that City.

Rabbit Ears Range:—Beginning near Rabbit Ears Pass, at the crest of the Park Range east of Steamboat Springs, and extending eastward for about 30 miles to a junction with the Front Range is the Rabbit Ears Range, a ridge of volcanic rock which separates North and Middle Parks. This three to six mile wide jumble of volcanic dikes and lava flows is cut by a series of necks and plugs marking the roots of old volcanoes. Dates obtained from these volcanic rocks range from Oligocene to Miocene, 32 to 22 m.y. ago, indicating a long period of activity.

Gore Range:—The Gore Range, a southeastward continuation of the Park Range, begins as a low ridge a few miles south of Gore Pass and trends southeastward for nearly 40 miles, ending at Tenmile Gorge. It is relatively narrow, varying in width from two to eight miles.

Like the Park Range, the Gore Range is an anticlinal fold, and it is bordered on the west by the Gore fault, which runs the full length of the Range. At the north end the fault is a thrust but in the southern two-thirds it is a high angle normal fault. This fault has been active at various times, beginning with the Precambrian.

The history of this Range is much like that of the Park Range. Both lie along the western edge of old Frontrangia, both received a thin sedimentary cover in the Mesozoic and both were uplifted in Laramide and late Cenozoic times. The major difference is that much of the uplift on the west flank of the Gore Range was along the Gore fault. Prolonged erosion has removed most of its former sedimentary cover leaving extensive exposures of Precambrian basement rocks.

Elevations in the Gore Range vary from a low of about 6,800 feet near Bond at the north end to 13,534 feet at Mt. Powell near the middle, and to 12,738 feet near the south end, just north of Vail Pass. Many peaks in this Range are unnamed and much of the area has been set aside as the Gore Range-Eagle's Nest Wilderness area.

Exploration for economic mineral deposits has resulted in only a few important discoveries. Most important of these is the mining district of Kokomo, noted for its past production of

Figure 23—Large igneous dike in Rabbit Ears Range

Figure 24—Gore Canyon at north end of Gore Range

copper, lead, zinc, silver and gold.

Near the north end of the Range is Gore Canyon, a steep-walled gorge of the Colorado River. This feature is considered to be one of the wild scenic spots of Colorado. At the south end of the Range is Tenmile Gorge, a deep canyon scoured out by large valley glaciers during the Pleistocene.

Tenmile Range:—South of Tenmile Creek the Park-Gore Range trend continues as the Tenmile Range. This thirteen mile long and six mile wide piece of rugged real estate is an asymmetric anticline with a gentle east flank and a steep, faulted west flank. Paleozoic sediments cover most of the Range, but granite is exposed at Quandary Peak (14,252 feet) near the south end and highest in the Range.

Mineral production of this Range has come largely from the east side of the Range in the Breckenridge district where base metal deposits (copper, lead, zinc, silver and gold) have been exploited periodically. Currently, the old mining area is a popular ski resort.

West Elk Mountains:—The West Elk Mountains are a 900 square mile area of volcanic terrain consisting mostly of the great mass of volcanic breccia, the West Elk Breccia. This material seems to have been derived from volcanoes which existed above large intrusives now exposed in the northern West Elks. Here, stocks, laccoliths, dikes and sills cut both lower Eocene sediments and the West Elk Breccia (35 to 30 m.y. old). To the south, near the Gunnison River, the West Elk Breccia coalesces with similar breccias of the same age derived from volcanoes in the northern and western San Juan Mountains. Great ash flow sheets (29 to 27 m.y. old), from calderas in the San Juans, overlie breccias from both areas.

The decipherable history of this area begins with the late Paleozoic when it formed the eastern edge of the Uncompahgre highland. Some 10,000 to 15,000 feet of sediment covered the old highland surface in the Mesozoic and early Cenozoic. In the Oligocene the Colorado mineral belt began to form with the intrusion of two batholiths, one of which rose sufficiently near the surface to feed volcanoes in the West Elk and San Juan

Figure 25—Tenmile Gorge near Frisco. Tenmile Range in background.

Figure 26—West Elk Breccia near Crawford. Note large blocks of volcanic debris.

Mountains. The resulting volcanic pile has been subjected to intermittent uplift as well as concentrated attacks by water and ice. Nevertheless, it remains a high, relatively inaccessible area with one peak (West Elk Peak) rising to 13,035 feet.

Mineral deposits are apparently scarce in these mountains but bituminous coal has been mined on the north and east flanks. Some of that on the east side is anthracite.

San Juan Mountains:—The largest group of mountains in Colorado are the San Juan Mountains located near the southern edge of Colorado West. They cover an area of more than 2,500 square miles in Colorado West and are composed largely of a thick sequence (up to 6,500 feet) of Tertiary volcanic rocks resulting from frequent eruptions of ash and lava from a series of volcanic vents.

The San Juans probably began in early Laramide time (about 72 m.y. ago) as an elongate domal uplift in an area coinciding in location with the southeastern part of the late Paleozoic Uncompahgria. Some intrusive and extrusive igneous activity occurred along the west side of the domal uplift at about the same time (70 to 69 m.y. ago). Erosion of Paleozoic and Mesozoic rocks from the crest of the dome continued until Oligocene time when there occurred widespread eruption of andesitic lavas from many volcanoes. These were especially active between 35 and 30 m.y. ago and they coalesced into a volcanic field covering much of the Southern Rocky Mountains. About 30 m.y. ago a major batholith worked its way up to shallow depths beneath the San Juans. Great pryoclastic eruptions occurred at various volcanic centers resulting in widespread silicic ash flows and related caldera subsidences. From 30 to 26.5 m.y. ago at least 17 large volume sheets of ash-flow tuff from at least 15 collapse craters spread across the area covering most,

Figure 27—Lost Lake near Somerset

Figure 28—Silverton and vicinity. Note broad glaciated valley in which town lies.

Figure 29—Red Mountain No's. 1 and 2. These altered rocks are within old Silverton caldera. Ghost town of Red Mountain in foreground.

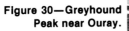
Figure 30—Greyhound Peak near Ouray.

if not all, of the old dissected dome. These calderas later (25 to 23 m.y. ago) became sites of renewed volcanic activity. During the caldera phase, numerous small stocklike masses of molten rock were intruded into sediments along the western and northeastern margins of the domal uplift to form satellite ranges, such as the San Miguel, Rico, La Plata, Cochetopa and LaGarita Mountains.

Since the volcanic phase, erosion has cut deep canyons into the volcanic pile producing such spectacular scenery that this area is commonly referred to as the Switzerland of America. Small areas of Precambrian basement rocks are exposed in deep canyons but the largest exposures are in the rugged Needle Mountains, which probably stood as high knobs during the pre-middle Cenozoic erosional phase and may have not been covered by ensuing volcanic eruptions. Most canyon walls exhibit thick sequences of Paleozoic and Mesozoic strata dipping outward from the old domal core and uncomformably overlain by Tertiary volcanic rocks.

In the Pleistocene (Ice Ages), valley glaciers occupied most of the drainages and modified them by deepening and smoothing

the valleys and narrowing the divides between adjacent valleys. The results can be seen in the numerous bowl-shaped depressions (cirques) at valley heads, narrow knife-like ridges (aretes) and low divides (cols), sharp angular peaks (horns and tinds, small glacial lakes (tarns), deep valleys with U-shaped cross sections, numerous high ridges of boulders mixed with clay and other rock fragments (lateral and end moraines composed of till), and paired terraces of outwash gravel along the lower parts of stream valleys. Studies show that ice formed in the higher areas and moved down the valleys at least three times—during Illinoisan time (Sacajawea Ridge glaciatian), during early Wisconsin time (Bull Lake glaciation) and during late Wisconsin time (Pinedale glaciation). Despite all this wear and tear there still remain some 13 peaks in the San Juans which exceed 14,000 feet in elevation. Included here are such towering giants as Wilson Peak, Windom Mountain, Mt. Sneffels, Sunshine Peak, San Luis Peak, Uncompahgre Peak, Redcloud Peak and Mt. Eolus.

Figure 31—Mesozoic and Cenozoic rocks exposed at Telluride.

The San Juan Mountains are the most highly mineralized region in Colorado. Some ore deposits formed in the Late Cretaceous, but most were emplaced during the Miocene, about 24.6 m.y. ago. Most of the ore is of the base metal type, consisting of minerals of gold, silver, copper, lead and zinc; but some fluorospar, barite, tungsten and uranium-vanadium deposits have also been mined. Principal mining districts include Sneffels, Red Mountain, Upper Uncompahgre (Ouray), Placerville, Mt. Wilson, Upper San Miguel (Telluride), Dunton, Ophir, Rico, LaPlata, Needle Mountain, Animas (Silverton), Eureka, and Galena (Lake City).

Scenic attractions include the Million Dollar Highway from Ouray to Durango, The Durango-Silverton narrow gauge railway, Lake San Cristobal and the Slumgullion debris flow near Lake City, and the numerous jeep trails to old mines and ghost towns.

Figure 32—Lizard Head Pass near Rico.

Intermediate Features:

Middle Park:—Middle Park is the south half of a Laramide structural and sedimentary basin which lies between the Front Range on the east and the Park Range on the west. It covers about 800 square miles and is bounded on the south by the northern terminations of the Vasquez and Williams River Ranges (prongs of the Front Range), and is separated from the north half of the basin (North Park) by the ridge of volcanics called the Rabbit Ears Range. Major attractions within this area are the hot springs, at the town of Hot Sulfur Springs, and the three lakes (Grand, Shadow Mountain and Grandby) along the eastern edge.

Four Corners Platform and Ute Mountain:—One of the lesser features of Colorado West, more or less intermediate between uplifts and downwarps, is the Four Corners platform extending southwestward from the San Juan mountains to the Four Corners area. It is bounded on the southeast by the San Juan basin and on the northwest by the Paradox basin and the

Figure 33—View across Middle Park. Sharp line at base of trees on top of mountain marks position of Williams Fork thrust fault. Precambrian rocks rest on Cretaceous shales.

Figure 34—Point Lookout at north end of Mesa Verde National Park.

Blanding basin. This area of approximately 2,000 square miles is a relatively stable area of nearly flat-lying strata interrupted only by the Ute Mountains (Sleeping Ute), a series of small stocks and associated laccoliths and sills intruded in Miocene(?) time. As a result of the intrusion, rocks in this part of the platform have been upwarped into an irregular domal feature. Breaching of this dome by erosion has revealed a core of igneous rocks surrounded by the upturned edges of the sediments into which they were injected. The highest elevation in the Ute Mountain area is Ute Peak at 9,977 feet. Much of this area is included within the Ute Mountain Indian Reservation.

Two of Colorado West's major attractions lie within this area, the geographical 'Four Corners' (the only place in the United States where four states meet—Colorado, New Mexico, Arizona and Utah) and Mesa Verde National Park, famed for its cliff dwellings and mesa top structures of masonry constructed by the ancient Anasazi (old ones), ancestors of the modern Pueblo Indians.

Others:—In addition to the intermediate areas previously discussed, there are six other minor features that should be

82

mentioned. Three of these are small projections of large basins extending into Colorado West from adjacent states—Uinta basin just west of Douglas arch, Blanding basin southwest of Paradox basin, and Chama basin at the southeast corner of the region. Two other features are sags or basins between uplifts—San Juan sag between the San Juan Mountains and the Gunnison uplift, and Carbondale basin between the Sawatch Mountains and White River uplift. The last is Archuleta anticlinorium, a series of closely spaced anticlines comprising an elevated region extending southeastward from the San Juan Mountains between the San Juan and Chama basins.

Figure 35—Cliff Palace at Mesa Verde National Park. Masonry structures of Pueblo III culture nestle in overhangs of Cretaceous Cliffhouse Sandstone.

Field Notes

Field Notes

PLANT
COMMUNITIES

PLANT COMMUNITIES

Colorado Deserts

Deserts are different—and that also includes the cold deserts of the lowest elevations in Colorado West. Our deserts are severe because temperatures can drop considerably below zero degrees fahrenheit with as much as several inches to a foot or more of snow in winter. In the summer the temperatures are reversed with long, hot days of over 100 degrees, low humidity and extreme drought conditions with low rainfall. It is easy to see that if any plant is to survive such adversity, it must adapt to these extremes.

It is surprising to note the numbers of plants that have become a part of this desert ecosystem. A few have adapted so well that they have become the dominant vegetation, not only of the barren saline slopes of western Colorado but all across the saline flats of the Great Basin to the west. Since the soils contain various types of salts, these are taken into some shrubby plants which are called, naturally enough, saltbush. Several types of saltbushes are native to our areas but the genus *Atriplex* is common to all of these species.

A variety of these saltbushes have common names like 4-wing saltbush (named for the four wings on the seeds), spiny saltbush (hard residual spines on the branch tips), mat saltbush for its prostrate nature, and so on. These and several others are common on the saline soils of Colorado West. Like the sagebrush community, these various types of saltbush are prominent in all of the intermountain areas of our west.

Other shrubs have their niche in this hot dry desert of Colorado. The drainage areas are characterized by grease-wood and, in some areas near water, *Tamarix* (salt cedar). Rabbitbrush, a beautiful yellow, fall blooming shrub, is very common, interspersed among the saltbushes of the desert and the sagebrush of higher elevations. Close observation during the spring on our desert will reveal a good variety of wildflowers. To name a few—cushion phlox, desert daisies, paintbrush, sego lily, and several species of the genus *Astragalus* (locally called locoweed). Yes, the desert is different and the desert can be beautiful!

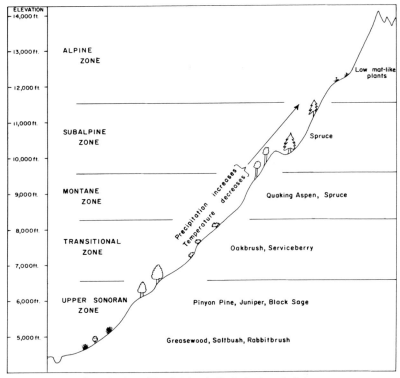

Generalized profile of Colorado West showing plant zones

Sagebrush Country

In many of the lower areas of Colorado West (Piceance basin, Sand Wash basin, San Juan basin, and the Gunnison and Colorado River valleys), the dominant vegetation is sagebrush [*Artemisia tridentata*]. Sometimes called big sagebrush or black sage, it is a shrubby range plant classed as an evergreen shrub ranging from two to ten feet tall or sometimes taller in rich deep soil. The genus *Artemisia* is not only the most abundant shrub in Colorado West but probably in all of western North America because it is very common in all of the intermountain region. At elevations from 6,000 to 8,000 feet one can find pure stands in hundreds of uninterrupted acres. Where soil depth is good and moisture is available, one can find areas of sage below 6,000 feet, and in warmer, more protected higher areas big sage occurs at elevations up to 10,000 feet. The species grows most vigorously in deep sandy loam of foothills and valleys. In fact, tall dense stands are indicative of fertile soil. But big sage grows on a variety of soils, even saline soils or on rocky outcrops. Present agricultural lands in western Colorado were developed from the big sagebrush areas of former years.

Colorado Desert

Leaves are a gray-green, narrow wedge shaped with three triangular teeth at the apex and are covered with many glandular tipped hairs which, when crushed, become very aromatic. It is for this reason that the term sage has been applied to these shrubs. *Artemisia* is not a true sage, instead it belongs to the composite family, most commonly characterized by the sunflower. The tan colored flowers are in terminal elongated clusters appearing in mid-to late summer. They are neither showy nor beautiful but are of value to some overwintering birds who feed on the seed heads.

Big sage is the most common species of the genus *Artemisia*, but there are several additional species which fill other niches in the western Colorado sagebrush ecosystem. Types such as fringed sage, silver sage, dwarf sage, low sage, spring sage and others grow only where specific elevation and soil conditions exist.

During spring and early summer one can find associated with these stands of sagebrush some of our lovely dryland wildflowers. Scarlet gilia, phlox, death camas, golden aster, hymenoxys, snakeweed and larkspur are only a few of the many perennials you will see as you explore the world of the underbrush.

Sagebrush

Pinyon-Juniper

The one lasting impression of western Colorado vegetation is the tremendous acreage of gnarled, shredded-barked junipers and the low, stunted pinyon. In many areas these pinyon-juniper stands are also mixed with sagebrush, especially where soil depths are good. But pinyon and juniper are hardy breeds and may blanket a steep, rocky slope or a dry, barren mesa top. There is beauty also in their gnarled branches for many tourists have been seen loading old weather-beaten limbs and trunks onto the tops of their cars to carry home for use as the center attraction of a decorative art piece.

This is that portion of Colorado where the deer hunter comes to bag his deer because animal life commonly abounds where two vastly different types of ecosystems meet, and where there is a change from one dominant type of plant life to another. In Colorado West the desert meets the mountains in this life zone, somewhat like the seacoast where the oceans meet the land.

An interesting change in vegetation can be observed in the plant world as we ascend in elevation from the desert floor to the mountain top, because most plants are quite limited to definite regions or life zones due to several important growth factors. In the juniper-pinyon belt these two trees represent the final climax stage of plant succession for the elevation of 5,000 to 6,500 feet, but in ideal situations they may be below that elevation or on dry sunny slopes they may be above the upper limit. In the spring a variety of wild flowers appear in the barren areas between the juniper and the pinyon. Commonly these flowers are the same as those in the sagebrush zone.

Juniper, sometimes called "cedar", can be recognized by its blue-green "berries" and small scale-like leaves. It has a refreshing odor which is particularly noticeable after a summer shower. Pinyon is a pine, bears two needles in each bundle and has cones. These trees are famous for their "pinyon nuts".

Pinyon-Juniper

Scrub Oak

Scrub Oak Brush

It is an interesting fact that when climbing up two thousand feet one encounters the same change in plant growth that he would find going north ten degrees in latitude. Thus, as we ascend to an elevation of approximately 6,500 feet in Colorado West, the vegetation begins to change from the dark green hued juniper-pinyon belt to the bright green of the broad-leafed scrub oak. This oak is *Quercus gambellii* which normally does not grow to tree size; but generally grows in dense thickets and stands eight to ten feet tall. It is not uncommon to see oak brush grow so thickly that no large animal is able to penetrate it.

Gambel oak covers much of the mountain slopes at approximately 7,000-8,500 feet in all of Colorado West. Sometimes along streams which course across this belt, one can find chokecherry and narrow leaf cottonwood associated with the oak. Occasionally, in more open areas, other shrubs such as rabbitbrush, big sage, mountain mahogany and serviceberry will be found. Serviceberry is easiest to identify in the spring because of the showy, profuse white blossoms.

Many grasses and flowering plants grow among the oakbrush in the dark soil formed over the years by decaying oak leaves. Look for lupine, mules ears, geranium, scarlet gilia, sweet vetch, sulphur flower, chickweed, penstemon and groundsel.

Gambel, or scrub oak, is easily recognized because of its lobed oak-like leaf and acorns. The Ute Indians reportedly burned off large areas periodically for ease of travel and to encourage deer browsing.

Aspen Groves

Populus tremuloides, most commonly known as quaking aspen or "quakie", is well known by most people of the United States. It grows all across the northern part of our country, along the Rocky Mountain chain, and is abundant on all Colorado West mountain slopes with elevations of 8,000-10,500 feet. These limits are somewhat arbitrary for one can find aspen groves in secluded seep areas below 8,000 feet and, at the other extreme, we can find aspen above the 10,500 foot level in sheltered areas away from the strong cold winter winds.

Aspen are truly beautiful and stately trees. In summer they are the epitome of coolness. Their white bark, dark green foliage quaking in the breeze and often times luxurious

Aspen Groves

undergrowth are inviting to the eye. And, as if their summer show is not enough, they again perform beautifully in the autumn with golden leaves and white bark against a background of blue sky. Probably more film has been spent on aspen in autumn than on any other tree or any other season.

Quaking aspen often form dense stands because they spread principally by roots. An entire grove could have originated from a single tree. Occasionally, one can find an older tree with dark rough bark in place of the smooth white bark, and some may be 90 feet tall and up to 30 inches in diameter.

Douglas fir and Engelmann spruce are commonly found growing with aspen; Douglas fir and spruce prefer moist shaded surroundings for young growth. Eventually, if the stand of aspen and evergreens are left long enough, the evergreens become the winner and crowd out the aspen.

Spruce Forests

Engelmann spruce [*Picea engelmanni*] may be found as far down as 8,500 feet on north-facing slopes where precipitation is somewhat greater-mostly from late melting snow; and at the other extreme at 11,500 feet in wind sheltered depressions hugging the terrain, even forming twisted, gnarled grotesque

Spruce

designs at timberline. Colorado West contains thousands of acres of almost uninterrupted spruce trees, some so crowded that trunk diameter is held to a minimum even though they may be several hundred years old. When allowed to grow in relatively rich soil and on flat or slightly rolling terrain, Engelmann spruce can be a stately tree. Two beautiful areas which have almost park-like settings of spruce and open meadows filled with summer wildflowers are the White River uplift between Glenwood Springs and Meeker, and Grand Mesa, a large high plateau east of Grand Junction.

Spruces are typical evergreens, that is they do not shed their leaves (needles) for several years (usually two or three years). Considering the fact that these living needles must withstand temperatures of 40 or 50 degrees below zero, with a chill factor which may drive the temperature considerably lower, one realizes how well adapted to the environment these clusters of living cells have become. Another classic example of plant adaptation!

Tramp through these spruce forests and get acquainted with some of the wildflowers and shrubs that grow in these densely shaded environments. Kinnikinnick (bearberry), Oregon grape, mountain lover and huckleberry are several low woody plants that are very common. The delicate jacobs ladder, solomon seal, deathcamas and arnica are a few of the many flowers that may be found in the dense shade or near the edge of a clearing.

Douglas fir, limber pine and bristlecone pine may be found in selected places within the spruce forest zone.

Alpine Tundra

"Tiptoe through the tundra" is an appropriate phrase for the delicate balance of nature which must be maintained in this extreme harsh environment. Like the desert, this area has low soil moisture, drying atmosphere, strong winds and exceptionally strong sunlight. Often also, the soil buildup is nil so that the plants grow on bare rock outcrops or at least very rocky ground. It is not wise to trample these areas for recovery of the vegetation comes slowly under such adverse conditions.

A stark landscape, however, is always especially beautiful. Study these plants closely and you can see some of the adaptations which each and every species has developed to protect itself from wind, sun or dessication. Notice how they

Tundra

hug the ground, some have a heavy wax (cuticle) buildup on the leaves, others are covered with profuse hairs, and all are programmed to grow rapidly as the snowline recedes to flower and to produce seeds during a very short period of time. Perhaps even in the midst of their growth peak in mid-July, they may be surrounded by freezing hail or covered with an early morning frost. Undaunted, they are able to continue their growth cycle thanks to these various adaptations.

Alpine meadows covered by wildflowers, clumps of grass and scattered boulders, all nestled among snowfields and peaks, are scenes of ultimate grandeur. The air is brisk, clear, and cool and crystal-like rivulets shimmer in the sunlight. Colorado is blessed with many miles of alpine terrain, much of it inaccessible to all but the heartiest of hikers. However, most of our major highways do get above timberline so that every traveler has a chance to see tundra at close range. Don't hurry past—get out of the vehicle and spend some time studying that arctic type vegetation, which includes such lovelies as the primrose, dryads, forget-me-not and buttercups, to name only a few. Truly, the tundra is unique!

DESERT WILDFLOWERS

SEGO LILY
(Mariposa Lily)

Calochortus nuttallii   Lily family

A more detailed description of this genus (but a different species) occurs in the section on mountain flowers. The desert variety is more commonly called Sego Lily than Mariposa Lily. Six white sepals and petals with six yellow stamens and a few curled slender green leaves are distinctive features of these plants. "Mariposa" means "butterfly" in Spanish, reflecting its attraction for these insects.

YUCCA

Yucca harrimaniae (neomexicana)   *Agave family*

This is a plant that is rather well known to everyone. It has several other familiar names such as Spanish Bayonet, Soapweed and Spanish Needle. The large candle of white, waxy flowers is so picturesque that it is often reproduced by artists and filmed by photographers as symbolic of the desert Southwest. It is the state flower of New Mexico.

WILD ONION

Allium textile   Lily family

Easily recognized for its onion-like odor by pinching the leaves and smelling the crushed foliage. Flower heads are light pink to white with several to many individual flowers comprising the umbel. Slender leaves are all basal and arise from a subterranean bulb. Desert onions are among the first to bloom in the spring. Seed heads are often already developed when most other spring flowers are in their prime.

Mariposa or Sego Lily

Yucca

Wild Onion

BLADDERSTEM
or
Desert Trumpet

Eriogonum inflatum   Buckwheat family

On the barren, gray desert slopes of western Colorado one may discover many strange inflated-stemmed plants in varying stages of development. The flowers are yellow, inconspicuous and at the tips of all the delicate branches. But the outstanding characteristic of the plant is the inflated stem which may be compounded with inflated stems on the secondary and tertiary branches. There is none other like it.

DESERT FOUR-O'CLOCK

Mirabilis glandulosa   Four-o'clock family

Vegetation of the desert four o'clock is quite different than other desert plants. The entire plant consists of a spreading clump, very stout and leafy. Leaves are quite large, dark green, cordate and opposite along the stem. Flowers are purplish-rose, showy and appear in clusters of six to eight within involucres at the apex of branches. The plant is somewhat viscid-glandular.

SAND VERBENA

Abronia elliptica   Four-o'clock family

Several to many white flowers are clustered in a head surrounded by five or more distinctive papery bracts. Each flower has a long tube and opens like a miniature funnel. Plants usually are decumbent (do not grow upright) and the leaves are opposite and somewhat thickened.

Desert Four-o-clock   **Bladderstem or Desert Trumpet**

Sand Verbena

YELLOW AND PINK BEEPLANT

Cleome lutea and C. serrulata   Caper family

Two very showy flowers within the same family and even the same genus. Yellow beeplant prefers hard clay and/or sand at approximately 4,500 feet; whereas, pink beeplant grows best in sandy soil. Both have four petals and six protruding, showy stamens. Our garden variety is called spiderplant. *Cleome*, sometimes called "skunk weed", yields a juice which was employed by early Pueblo Indians for making black designs on pottery.

LAVENDER MUSTARD

Sisymbrium elegans (Thelypodiopsis elegans)   Mustard family

A very early blooming pink-lavender mustard averaging two to three feet tall, depending on spring moisture. Four petals, six stamens and a superior ovary denote the mustard family. Long slender siliques contain many seeds.

PEPPERWEED

Lepidium montanum   Mustard family

Mustards are very common among early blooming desert widlflowers. Older plants of pepperweeds (they are perennial) are multibranched and many flowered, growing one to two feet tall, depending on soil type and moisture. White blossoms of pepperweed are rather conspicuous among grasses and desert shrubs. Each small blossom has the four sepal, four petal, six stamen and one pistil combination of the mustard family. Seed pods are short, rounded and flat.

106

Yellow Beeplant

Pink Beeplant

Lavender Mustard

Pepperweed

TWIN BLADDER POD

Physaria acutifolia   Mustard family

A common, low-growing early blooming plant with bright yellow flowers. Since this is a mustard, look for four sepals, four petals and six stamens. The distinctive feature is the double bladder design of the maturing ovary. Leaves are silvery and spatulate.

DESERT PLUME
and
Princes Plume

Stanleya albescens and S. pinnata   Mustard family

Identified by four yellow petals, six prominent stamens and superior ovary. These two species are easily separated on the basis of floral color. Desert Plume is light faded lemon yellow and grows on barren gray shale. Leaves are a bluish cast. Princes Plume is a bright conspicuous yellow and the plants grow among sandstone boulders or on sandy pediments. Leaves are deep green.

Twin Bladder Pod

Desert Plume   **Princes Plume**

LOCOWEEDS

Astragalus amphioxus, et. al.   Pea family

There are several different species of this genus; and, along with some plants of the genus *Oxytropis*, are called locoweed by the natives. Two important features set these plants apart as members of the pea family—the pinnately compound leaves (which many pea members have) and the flower (an upright banner, two side wings and a keel, collectively forming five petals).

Sphaeralcea parvifolia
and   **POPPYMALLOW**
Sphaeralcea coccinea   Mallow family

This plant has a broad range of elevation in Colorado from 4,500 to 6,500 feet. The showy tomato-red flowers occur along elongated racemes and may stand two feet tall. These are typical hollyhock blossoms when inspected closely for the column of light yellow anthers are fused and completely encircle the pistil. The two common species may be separated on the basis of leaf design. *S. coccinea* has dissected leaves and *S. parvifolia* has more geranium-type leaves. Both are common on the lowest part of the desert.

Locoweed

Poppymallow

Poppymallow

CACTUS

Colorado has four distinct types of this plant family which has adapted so well to the desert environment.

Opuntia (prickly pear) has stems in joints.

Coryphantha (mammillaria) has spine clusters at the tips of nipple-like projections of the stem.

Echinocactus (barrel) has blossoms at the apex of the fleshy stem and floral tube in the spring.

Echonocereus (hedgehog) has blossoms in a circle around the apex of the stem and the flowers have a spiny outer floral tube.

Opuntia (Prickly Pear) Cactus

Mammillaria Cactus

Echinocactus (Barrel)

Hedgehog Cactus

EVENING PRIMROSE

Oenothera caespitosa   Evening primrose family

A large delicate white four-petaled flower that fades pink when old and withered. It usually closes at night. Prefers open rocky outcrops and is prevalent around edge of ant hills on the desert floor.

DESERT PARSLEY

Cympoterus fendleri and *C. bulbosus*   Parsnip or Carrot family

One of our earliest flowers on the desert. Desert Parsleys are easy to identify because the leaves are very much parsley- or carrot-like. The yellow or purple flower cluster hugs the ground with a dark shiny green rosette of leaves. Individual flowers are very tiny but in clusters of tiny umbels they become showy. A more detailed discussion of individual flowers in this family is included in the mountain flower section.

DESERT PHLOX and PINK PHLOX

Phlox hoodii and *P. longifolia*   Phlox family

Five showy white to pink to lavender radiating petals with a small rounded throat into which project five stamens. These are the most distinctive features of the Phlox plants. *P. hoodii* forms a low tough mat with sharp pointed leaves (vegetation resembles a moss) and *P. longifolia* is taller, occurring either in a small loose cluster or singly with or under sage plants.

Evening Primrose

Fendler's Parsley

Desert Parsley

Desert Phlox

Pink Phlox

SCORPION WEED
or
Wild Heliotrope

Phacelia corrugata and *P. splendens*   Waterleaf family

Dark blue-violet, open bell shaped flowers with five conspicuous yellow anthers at the tips of protruding stamens. The inflorescence is a terminal curved raceme and flowers are born only along one side (scorpioid). Most leaves are basal, flowers are annuals.

YELLOW BORAGE and WHITE BORAGE

Cryptantha flava and C. flavoculata   Borage family

Most of the desert borages are covered with sharp hairs and feel quite coarse to the touch. Chracteristically one stalk gives rise to a cluster of flowers at its tip. Both yellow and white species have five showy petals united to form an elongated tubular base. At the central throat of the flowers are five raised crests called corona which hide the stamens from obvious view. The white borage may be a foot high in more moist years, but the yellow borage makes up for its smaller stature by a larger flower head.

Scorpion Weed or Wild Heliotrope

Yellow Borage

White Borage

PENSTEMON

Penstemon moffattii   Figwort family

Penstemons in Colorado are plentiful and several others are described in this book with the mountain flowers. *P. moffattii* is one of these hardy perennials which can be found in early spring on the warm desert floor. Deep blue throated flowers in a raceme and heights up to six or eight inches depending on spring rains. They will be with Sego lilies, wild onions and paperflowers.

PAINTBRUSH

Castilleja chromosa   Figwort family

The only bright scarlet-red flowers on the desert. Prefers sandy ground among grasses and varied shrubs. The true petals are green hornlike projections; whereas, the red "petals" are really highly colored subtending leaves. For further description of floral parts, see discussion under mountain flowers.

DAISY

Erigeron utahensis, E. pumilus, E. flagellaris   Sunflower family

Several daisies are present within the desert basin and on its flanks. These listed are three of the more common species. All are white and yellow flowered. Most members of the sunflower family are easily identified because of the presence of disc and ray flowers.

Penstemon

Paintbrush

Daisy Utahensis

ASTERS

Leucelene ericoides and *Machaeranthera venusta (Xylorhiza venusta)*   Sunflower family

Most asters are shades of white, pink or lavender-purple and often bloom the latter part of the growing season. They are easy to identify because they have the disc and ray flowers so typical of our garden asters and daisies. Golden asters, which are not true asters, are discussed as *Heterotheca villosa* on a later page.

ACTINEA

Hymenoxys acaulis (Tetraneuris ivesiana)   Sunflower family

Bright yellow disc and ray flowers. No leaves on the stems, and a rosette of leaves at the base. All the leaves are linear, entire margined and densely hairy.

DESERT DANDELION

Malacothrix sonchoides   Sunflower family

Bright yellow flowers—all ray, no disc flowers are present. This plant stands about six to eight inches tall in good years, has a few linear stem leaves and a basal rosette of leaves all pinnatified (as in dandelion). The main axis may be branched. Plants are annual.

Aster

Actinea

Desert Dandelion

PAPERFLOWER

Psilotrophe bakeri   Sunflower family

Both disc and ray flowers are bright yellow. Grows as a low spreading perennial cluster with many upright blooms. An established plant may have twenty or more individual stems each topped with flowers. Leaves are mostly basal and woolly.

GOLDENWEED

Haplopappus armerioides (Stenotus armerioides)   Sunflower family

Bright yellow disc and ray flowers. Perennial plants growing from stout woody established clumps. Leaves are entire margined, smooth surfaced and linear. Bracts around the flower head are in three-four series, erect, stiff, greenish at the tip and somewhat sticky-glandular.

Paperflower

Goldenweed

WILD CHRYSANTHEMUM

Platyschkuhria integrifolia (Bahia nudicaulis)   Sunflower family

Usually one or two bright yellow disc and ray flowers at the tip of ten to twelve inch stems. Leaves are entire margined, lanceolate and mostly basal. Only a few reduced stem leaves may be present. Perennial plants grow from woody bases. They are about the same height as *Actinea* but *Bahia* may have reduced stem leaves and more than one flower head per stem.

CREAM TIPS

Hymenopappus filifolius   Sunflower family

Small light yellow to cream colored disc flowers from much-branched perennial herbaceous plants. Leaves mostly crowded near the base and once or twice divided into small linear divisions. Leaves and stems are gray due to many fine kinky hairs.

DESERT YARROW

Chaenactis stevioides   Sunflower family

Small heads of white disc flowers only. Annual plants, usually a foot or more tall and branched. Stems are leafy. Leaf is divided into small linear segments.

Wild Chrysanthemum

Cream Tips

Desert Yarrow

GAILLARDIA

Gaillardia pinnatifida   Sunflower family

Although many of the sunflower members have both disc and ray flowers colored yellow, and are therefore hard to separate, Gaillardia is easily differentiated because the disc flowers are reddish-purple and the rays are yellow to reddish. Gaillardias prefer sandy ground.

TOWNSENDIA

Townsendia incana   Sunflower family

Flowers are pale lavender-blue with a yellow center of disc flowers appearing in early spring. Plants are hard to find because they form small cushion-like clusters hugging the desert floor. The plant appears to have little or no stem and the leaves are crowded together forming a compacted rosette.

DESERT PINK

Lygodesmia grandiflora   Sunflower family

Because the pink flowers look like annual Dianthus (pinks) that we grow in our home flower gardens, these dainty desert types were given that same name. The similarity is only superficial, however, for we are talking about two different plant families. Desert pinks are commonly scattered among the desert saltbushes.

Gaillardia

Townsendia

Desert Pink

MOUNTAIN
WILDFLOWERS

DOGTOOTH VIOLET

Erythronium grandiflorum   Lily family

Not a violet but a lily and for that reason perhaps the lesser known name of snowlily is much more appropriate. The latter name is also more ideal because these flowers are blooming while snowbanks lie nearby. They generally are in full bloom from the middle to the latter part of June at elevations around 10,000 feet.

This is a beautiful flower averaging six to eight inches high with pendant yellow blossoms of recurved sepals and petals. There are three sepals and three petals all alike, which makes it appear as though all six stamens (male part of the flower) protrude from the floral throat, adding to its delicate beauty.

Leaves in dogtooth violet (snowlily) add considerably to the overall picture of this plant. Like the slender smooth floral stalk, the two long lanceolate leaves arise from the basal bulb, and they stand erect in a fresh flower, sometimes nearly equal to the height of the lily blossom. The entire effect is one of graceful lines and symmetry.

MARIPOSA or SEGO LILY

Calochortus gunnisonii   Lily family

"Consider the lilies of the field" related the Psalmist of old, and rightly so, for in the acres of rolling open meadows of our higher regions one should stop and consider the lily. Ours is mariposa lily or also frequently called sego lily. These lilies bloom in late May in the lower desert areas of Colorado West. The species at the lower elevation is *nuttalli* but the generic name is the same for these two types which grow in such widely different environments.

Flowers are typically lily- or tulip-like with three sepals and three petals all alike in color and texture. The throat of the flower is colored purple-brown and contains six stamens, each with long slender yellow anthers. Flowers arise singly or in groups of two to three from a single bulb.

The several leaves are grass-like and sometimes die back before the flowers appear. They resemble the nodding onion leaves which are growing in the same meadows. A pinch of the leaves and a smell of the fingers will quickly help you to decide the difference.

Mariposa lily is the state flower of Utah.

Dogtooth Violet

Sego Lily

FALSE SOLOMONSEAL

Smilacina racemosa
Smilacina stellata   Lily family

Also called solomonsplume, the two different species of the genus *Smilacina* are delicate looking plants with flowers in terminal racemes [*S. stellata*] or panicles [*S. racemosa*]. Flowers are cream-white with both sepals and petals forming the six-pointed star floral pattern. Since false solomonseal is in the Lily family, the three outer petal-like floral parts are sepals but are equally as showy (white or beautifully colored) as the petals. Stamens are six in number and are quite conspicuous with their projecting yellow anthers.

False solomonseal is usually growing in open meadows or at the edge of spruce stands. They develop from horizontal rootstocks so that they may occur in groups. The unbranched stems, which average about a foot in height, are leafy with alternate leaves showing pronounced parallel veins. This type of venation is typical of Lily family.

The fruit is a berry, in *S. racemosa* red speckled with purple and in *S. stellata* purplish-black.

TWISTED STALK

Streptopus amplexifolius   Lily family

Common floral names may or may not give an indication of some distinctive feature about the plant; but the peculiarity of a twisted flower stalk was significant enough to warrant giving that name to this species.

Floral features are similar to all members of the Lily family—three sepals and three petals (greenish-white), six stamens and a single pistil. Flowers appear very dainty with their slightly recurved tips and slender pendant blossoms. They arise solitary or occasionally two together from the axis of stem and leaf.

Fruits are equally attractive later in the summer when they ripen into shiny red berries.

Twisted stalk may appear to be very similar to the two false solomon seals because their leaves are ovate to ovate-lanceolate and arise opposite along the stem. However, twisted stalk flowers are born in axillary positions rather than in a panicle or raceme at the top of the axis.

Look for twisted stalk in about the same place as false solomonseal. It enjoys deeply shaded areas mainly under aspen in rich soil. Blooming time is early to mid-July.

False Solomonseal

False Solomonseal

Twisted Stalk

MOUNTAIN DEATHCAMAS
(Wandlily)

Zygadenus elegans   Lily family

The name deathcamas for a flower sounds very ominous. It really should be the name of a poisonous mushroom. Our mountain deathcamas is only mildly poisonous but some of the species in other areas of the United States are quite poisonous to livestock. Perhaps wandlily would be a more appropriate name for this dainty cream colored flower.

Like all lilies there are three sepals and three petals arising nearly on the same level. The six floral parts are all alike in texture and color. They bear a bilobed green patch at their base. Six stamens project out from the floral base and are quite showy when the tiny flower is fresh.

Leaves are all basal, slender and elongated. They resemble some of the wild onions but a pinch of the leaves and a smell of the fingers could easily separate these two plants for any amateur.

Wandlily can be found in bog areas and along sluggish streams. They prefer open moist meadows or at edge of aspen groves if said area is bog-like.

NODDING ONION

Allium cernuum   Lily Family

One would hardly believe that the onion would be one of the common wildflowers of the Rocky Mountains. We usually do not associate onion odor with beautiful flowers. If ever in doubt on an onion blossom just pinch the leaves and smell your fingers. It provides just about the easiest and most accurate clue one could devise for floral identification.

These delicate deep rose colored blossom clusters (on umbels) are plentiful in open grassy meadows. They appear during mid-summer in areas where outcrops and boulders are common in association with dark soil.

Allium is not a tall plant (about six-eight inches high) but it is very showy. A single flower stalk may arise from the basal bulb or several flowering stalks may be clustered together. All slender, grass-like parallel-veined leaves arise from the bulb. They may dry and wither before the flower head opens.

Individual flowers are typical of lily family characteristics. The three sepals and three petals are all alike both in color and texture. The six stamens protrude from the partially closed petals. Individual flowers are pendant, thus the name of nodding onion.

**Mountain Deathcamas
(Wand Lily)**

Nodding Onion

FALSE HELLEBORE

Veratrum tenuipetalum   Lily family

This plant is often called skunk cabbage, but false hellebore and skunk cabbage do not share the same family. In fact, skunk cabbage is not found in this area. It is good to get acquainted with false hellebore for it is one of the tallest and most conspicuous wildflowers. It averages four feet tall, growing profusely in moist rich soil in thick clumps. It is conspicuous for its large stalks and many broad clasping leaves which are strongly veined. The veins are rounded and heavily ribbed giving the leaf blade a pleated look.

At the tip of the unbranched stalk arises the panicle of numerous whitish to light green flowers. When fully developed the inflorescence may add a foot or more to the entire plant height.

Individual flowers have the three sepals and three petals alike and all are "petaloid". Six stamens project from the floral throat.

False hellebore often occurs in such dense stands that no other plant is able to penetrate the dense foliage to compete with it. They form thick rootstocks.

IRIS

Iris missouriensis   Iris family

Most everyone can recognize this flower as one closely related to the cultivated iris in our own gardens. The flowers are large, light blue, with three petals pointed upward and three sepals recurved downward. The roots are large and fleshy and spread by creeping underground rootstocks. Since several of these blossoming stems may arise from one large fleshy rootstock it is understandable that one may find Rocky Mountain iris in dense stands in moist meadows. Iris are hardy plants and in some places they have encroached upon the gravelly dry slopes of the highway.

A close inspection of the flower reveals that the outer floral whorl of threes, which are recurved, are the sepals and the inner whorl of threes are the upright more slender petals. Also, there are three colored, petal-like styles which arch over and cover the yellow stamens. Thus, unlike most flowers, the stamens in the iris are not noticeable.

Leaves are flat, elongated, and taper to a point like a long sword.

False Hellebore

Iris

FAIRY SLIPPER

Calypso bulbosa   Orchid family

Some of our Colorado West wildflowers are not abundant and one of the loveliest ones, which could be in danger of extinction, is Fairy Slipper. Like Bog Orchid and Coral Root, this dainty pink orchid is small, selective in growth habit and can be easily overlooked.

One solitary flower blooms at the tip of a stem that arises from a tuber or enlarged bulb-like structure (hence species name, *bulbosa*). Usually one leaf is present although sometimes it has dried before the flower blooms.

The enlarged "slipper" (a petal) is light pink with brown dots and contains a beard of yellow hairs. The other two petals and the three sepals are alike—a medium rose and pointed at the tips. Because the flower is so distinctive, one has little trouble in identification.

Fairy slippers are not common so when a cluster is encountered, please leave them for others to enjoy. Look for them in boggy areas, near seeps and springs at elevations of 8,000-10,000 feet in late May through June, depending on elevation. They prefer well shaded areas in moist deep black soil with rotting logs or other plant debris.

Calypso (the genus name) refers to the nymph that detained Odysseus seven years on his journey home from Troy.

BOG ORCHID and CORAL ROOT

Habenaria hyperborea
and
Corallorhiza maculata   Orchid Family

Even though our Colorado orchids are not large and showy, they are just as beautiful as any found in the tropics. However, because of their small size and growth habits, they are seldom observed. As the name implies this greenish flowered orchid grows in bog areas of old filled lake beds or stream channels and in seep areas where water stands in small pools. Mid-July is a good time to look for this orchid. Another orchid, coral root [*Corallorhiza maculata*] is also found in our mountains. Look for it in moist areas along small streams in shadowy aspen groves. It will be quite well hidden among the other herbaceous undergrowth. Coral root is pink with darker pink spots on the enlarged white lower lip. The three sepals and the two erect petals have a pink cast. It has no leaves; just the slender dark pink to wine colored stalk that bears the flower axis.

Bog orchid has lanceolate leaves arising from tuberous, thickened roots. The flowers have three green sepals and three lighter green petals. The upper enlarged sepal forms a hood for two of the incurved petals. They appear to make an archway inside the sepal.

Flowers are quite numerous along the raceme and exude a delicate fragrance.

Fairy Slipper

Bog Orchid

Coral Root

BISTORT

Bistorta (Polygonum) bistortoides   Buckwheat family

This white to light pink cluster of many small flowers arises at the tip of a slender, smooth stalk. Stems average twelve inches tall. The large, lanceolate leaves are all basal with an occasional small leaf along the single flowering stalk.

Bistort thrives in open meadows competing with the perennial grasses and other mid-summer flowers. There is no mistaking it for any other wild flower while in the meadows during mid summer, for none have its solitary terminal inflorescence.

A close look at the individual flower gives us an insight into the Buckwheat family. There are no petals, rather the five sepals become petal-like. There are eight stamens and the tiny ovary is superior. At the base of each small white flower is a brown bract.

This family includes some common weeds, such as knotweed and dock. Rhubarb, often grown in our gardens for use in sauce and pies, is also in this family.

MOUNTAIN SORREL

Oxyria digyna   Buckwheat family

A plant that looks very much like dock (same family) except that the leaves are rounded instead of lanceloate and they tend to form a low mound. There are many greenish petals but the sepals are tinged with red. It is the collection of minute sepals, therefore, that give the inflorescence its color. Flowers arise on a conspicuously upright raceme which may be eight or ten inches long. The flowers are very tiny and inconspicuous. It is the broadly winged rose colored fruits that make the flower so attractive.

General features of mountain sorrel flowers are the same as bistort. Both of these wildflowers are in the Buckwheat family. This family is not noted for individual floral size. Some of the details regarding floral characteristics have been covered more thoroughly in the discussion on Bistort.

Mountain sorrel is a perennial plant with thick fleshy taproots. Leaves are mostly basal and, since they are slightly acid, may add flavor to a sandwich, be used as greens, or cooked with vegetables. Try some next time you are having a picnic in the mountains.

Sorrel prefers open sunny locations near rocks where summer rains may produce a little additional moisture.

Just because this plant belongs to the dock family, don't look for it to be so large and husky as the common dock seen nearly everywhere in the mountains.

Bistort
Mountain Sorrel

UMBRELLA PLANT and SULPHUR FLOWER

Eriogonum umbellatum (Sulphur Flower)
and
Eriogonum subalpinum (Umbrella Plant)   Buckwheat family

In order to see a single flower of either of these two plants you would have to employ a hand lens or, even better, binocular scope with about 50x magnification. So the old adage of strength in numbers becomes of great importance to the umbrella plant and sulphur flower.

A single flower has six minute sepals and no petals. There are several stamens and a tri-parted stigma and style. Numerous flowers are crowded together on an umbrella shaped cluster arising on short stalklets. Several of these cluster cups are congregated at the tips of several stalks (pedicels) which arise from a common point. These pedicels are subtended by leaf-like bracts. The leafless stem (scape) that bears the flowers is often eight inches tall.

Inflorescences of these two Eriogonums dry with the sepals remaining intact. Umbrella plant dries to a pinkish color and sulphur flower dries orange-yellow. They make very lovely specimens for winter bouquets.

These two Eriogonums are abundant in open rather rocky or boulder strewn ground in mid-July.

Umbrella Plant

Sulphur Flower

CHICKWEED

Cerastium arvense   Pink family

At elevations of 9,000-10,000 feet among rocky outcrops where drainage is good, one is likely to encounter the low-growing chickweed. It blooms mid-to late July and August and is associated with other plants which tolerate rocky ground with little or no topsoil. Kingscrown, rosecrown, pink and white pussytoes, rose and yellow paintbrush, violets and other low growing perennials are all found in association with chickweed.

By the time chickweed is blooming wild candytuft has gone to seed so there is no duplication of showy white flowers in these same open meadows.

There are two outstanding features which may aid in identification of chickweed. Each of the five white petals is deeply cleft and, unless one inspects the flower closely, it might appear to have ten petals. Because of this deep lobing of the petals some species are called mouse-ear chickweed.

The other distinctive feature of chickweed is opposite entire margined lanceolate leaves with a slight swelling at the node (junction of leaf with stem).

Some chickweed of the genus *Stellaria* are also found in Colorado West mountains.

PONDLILY

Nuphar polysepalum (Nuphar luteus ssp. *polysepalum)*   Waterlily family

From mid-July to the latter part of the summer one can find pondlilies in small lakes that are usually no more than three to four feet deep at the middle. The edge of the ponds where the pondlilies grow are often no more than two feet deep. These are lakes that are gradually filling with sediment and decaying plant debris. Rhizomes of pondlilies thrive on silt-laden muddy bottoms of these shallow lakes. The large floating or sometimes slightly elevated oval leaves are attached to the rootstocks by long petioles. From a distance the leaves are very conspicuous.

Flowers are strikingly different than any other discussed in this book because one waxy yellow flower may be two to three inches wide. Petals and sepals are both brightly colored. The sepals may have a tint of green on the outside; and, as the flower ages, shades of red develop on the edge and outside of the petals. Stamens are numerous (pondlily is a primitive flower) and the strikingly designed disc-like stigma looks like a large yellow button in the middle of the flower.

It would be well worth the walk to go down to one of these lakes and inspect this pondlily closely.

Chickweed

Pondlily

GLOBEFLOWER

Trollius laxus   Buttercup or Crowfoot family

White flowers, averaging one to one and a half inches across, make globeflower one of more conspicuous early blooming species in the mountains. It enjoys the more moist areas of meadows near melting snow banks, along streams and under spruce (in less dense stands).

In the globeflower, as in a few other types of flowers mentioned in this book, the five to eight sepals are the showy petal-like parts which become the flower, and the petals are reduced to small, white remnants between the sepals and stamens. The yellow stamens are numerous and produce a sunburst effect. Several light green pistils form the center of this showy flower, which gradually acquires a brownish parchment look with age.

Leaves are palmately divided with five to seven lobes and toothed margins. They are massed below the flowers so that as one looks down on a cluster of globeflower the divided green leaves make an appropriate background.

These flowers are not to be confused with marsh marigold or alpine anemone. All three are in the same family, enjoy moist swampy environment, but only marsh marigold and globeflower bloom in early summer. Probably the palmately lobed leaves of globeflower and the rounded single blade of the marsh marigold would be best criteria for separation of these two. Alpine anemone's later summer bloom would easily separate it.

MARSH MARIGOLD

Caltha leptosepala   Crowfoot family

These are large white flowers, sometimes one and one-half inches across, with many yellow stamens forming a yellow center. Marsh marigold, also called elkslip, grows profusely in moist meadows, along streams, and around lakes. It is an early summer bloomer, beginning in late June at lower elevations and continuing until late July at higher elevations. The under side of the petal-like white structures have a bluish cast. Even though these white parts of the flower look like petals, they are not petals but sepals. The sepals in many flowers are green and inconspicuous so that one does not become as familiar with the term sepal as he does with the word petal.

The leaves are also distinctive with their dark waxy green oval design and a heart-shaped base. All leaves and flowers are basal.

There are many separate pistils clustered with the yellow stamens in the center of the flower. These pistils mature into elongated green follicles (pod-like structures).

Do not confuse marsh marigold, globeflower and alpine anemone. Read the description of each to clarify the right genus.

Globeflower

Marsh Marigold

ALPINE ANEMONE

Anemone narcissiflora ssp. *zephra*   Crowfoot family

There are several species of anemones in our state at various elevations but few are as showy as alpine anemone. Look for this conspicuous white flower with the yellow stamen center in the higher mountains at approximately 10,000 feet. It will be growing in deeper soil around shrubs, mainly willows. Some plants will stand a foot or more tall when blooming so that they are easily recognized, even from a distance. The flowers resemble those of globeflower, but notice that the basal leaves and smaller stem leaves are deeply parted and again cleft so that they appear as many linear divisions. Another flower with which one may be confused is marsh marigold; but this plant likes wet ponds and swamp areas and has an oval design with a heart shaped base to the leaves.

"Anemone" means "wind" in Greek which accounts for the common name for all members of this genus—windflowers.

The Romans used some species as treatment for malaria and the American Indians used the roots in the treatment of wounds. It was to have had certain mystical powers.

PASQUE FLOWER

Pulsatilla patens   Crowfoot family

Like the crocus of our home gardens, this lead-blue, tulip-like flower is certainly a harbinger of spring in our Colorado West mountains. Even before the snows are gone the leaves and bud will poke through the crust; or it will be blooming in the midst of a late spring snow. So you must be in the mountains early to see this one!

This beauty may have the title of "plant with most common names" for many old timers know the pasque flower as mayflower, wild crocus, wild tulip, hartshorn, Easter flower, etc. Also, botanists have had difficulty in establishing a genus and species name. It has been labeled *Pulsatilla ludoviciana*, *Anemone patens*, etc. But a pasque flower by any other name is still beautiful. They are easy to identify, not only because they may be the only flower blooming besides the pink spring beauty, but because the upper whorl of bracts (leaf-like) on the stem are divided into narrow, hairy lobes; yellow stamens are numerous, and the five-seven sepals are showy—usually an inch or more long. There are no petals. Basal leaves are also much divided but are usually not well developed while flowers are blooming.

Fully developed leaves and the many long feathery tails on the achenes ("seeds") are later evidence of where pasque flowers once bloomed.

148

Alpine Anemone

Pasque Flower

DELPHINIUM

Delphinium barbeyi   Crowfoot family

This is a tall perennial averaging three to five feet high when in full bloom. It usually stands above the other flowers in its environment. In the Colorado West mountains it is one of the dominant flowers from the middle to the latter part of July, occurring in open meadows or in association with low shrubs. The palmately veined leaves very much resemble those of geraniums, but the leaf margins are more deeply cleft than those of geranium.

The flower stalks (racemes) range between one and two feet long with deep blue, almost black-blue irregular flowers. Common perennial delphinium grown in our flower gardens may be white, light blue, shades of darker blue or even pinks.

The five sepals in an individual flower are larger and more showy than the petals. The upper sepal projects backward into a long spur showing that it is an irregular flower. The petals are small and in two sets of two petals each. The upper two formed into the spur are white tipped, the lower two are clawed and blue. There are many stamens in each flower.

There are healthy stands of delphinium in all meadows of the Colorado West mountains from the Rabbit Ears pass area on the north to the slopes of the San Juans.

LARKSPUR

Delphinium nelsonii (D. nuttallianum)   Crowfoot family

Larkspur is another of the lovely delphinium genera but it blooms earlier in the summer and is much shorter. Floral color is such a beautiful piercing blue that even though they may not grow any taller than one to one and a half feet one can easily spot them in the grassy openings and marginal aspen areas where they grow. They are also common along the roadways at elevations between 8,000 and 10,000 feet. Seldom do these plants occur in close proximity to one another; usually occurring as solitary individuals sprinkled among clumps of grass and other flowers.

Typical of the floral structure of delphinium are the five conspicuous sepals with the upper sepal projecting backward into a long spur. This is different than in the columbine in which the five petals form the spurs rather than the sepals. The petals in larkspur are four in number, inconspicuous and nearly white.

The leaves of this plant are palmately veined and more deeply dissected between these large veins than in the delphinium.

Most laymen apply the name larkspur to the annual garden delphinium and refer to the perennial variety as delphinium.

Delphinium

Larkspur

COLUMBINE

Aquilegia caerulea
and
Aquilegia elegantula   Crowfoot family

This delicate, showy perennial is certainly one flower to which no Coloradan need be introduced. Since it is the state flower of Colorado it has been photographed more and discussed more in laymen magazines than any other of our wildflowers.

Columbines may be found in moist, shaded wood areas under aspen and spruce or in open meadows crowded closely with many other perennial types. Sometimes the blue of the five sepals becomes pale blue or even white. It may be noted that generally the flowers in deep shade have the bluest color and those in full sunlight most of the daylight hours are quite pale to white.

The five petals form the characteristic spurs which so easily identify the columbine.

A columbine with yellow sepals and red spurred petals (*A. elegantula*) is also present in our mountains, but not in as great profusion as the blue species (*A. caerulea*). However, since this red columbine is such a striking flower it is also pictured here. It may be found in approximately the same environment as *A. caerulea*.

MONKSHOOD

Aconitum columbianum   Crowfoot family

When walking through moist aspen groves or along small streams about mid-July you should encounter some tall dark purple flowered monkshood. They may stand three to four feet tall when in full bloom. In early August monkshood may be found in moist areas of the open meadows at slightly higher elevations (around 10,000 feet). They are an unusual flower because the upper sepals (the petals in monkshood are minute or lacking) project up and then arch over the other floral parts forming a hood. Monkshood is an old English name for this flower since, apparently to some Englishmen, it resembled the hood worn by some monks.

There are four other sepals in monkshood but only the two side ones are obvious; the lower two are small.

The entire flower stalk is a raceme with the individual flower arising along an axis. In dense shade these flowers may be few in number along the stem. For that reason monkshood may be a little harder to find. In the more open moist areas the blossoms are more dense.

Leaves are palmately three to five lobed, each lobe cleft and toothed, very typical of the Crowfoot family.

Columbine

Columbine

Monkshood

BUTTERCUP

Ranunculus alismaefolius   Crowfoot family

Buttercup is a well known flower abundant in moist meadows and marshy areas throughout the continental United States. There are about forty known species, and the Rocky Mountain area has its fair share of these. The species described here is common during early and midsummer in our mountains adding its bright yellow color to the flowering landscape. The ten petals have a waxy yellow appearance, almost as though they have been varnished. There are many stamens and many separate pistils all crowded on a tiny conical base (receptacle).

Leaves are oval to lanceolate with slightly denticulate margins (may be entire). There is much variation in the design of the leaf between the various species of buttercups in the Rocky Mountain region. Buttercups could be confused with cinquefoil but upon close inspection of the design of the receptacle (conical base, from which floral parts arise, as compared to saucer-shaped base) the two can be differentiated. Also, the yellow of the petals is more waxy appearing in buttercup than are the petals of cinquefoil (*Potentilla*).

SUGARBOWL

Clematis hirsutissima   Crowfoot family

One look at this flower and you can see a resemblance to an old fashioned sugarbowl with the wide rim. Sugarbowl is deep purple inside and light purple outside. The outside is densely hairy and the hairs do not allow the deep purple color to appear as it does on the inside.

As in globeflower and marsh marigold these showy purple structures are sepals and not petals. Sepals are the lowest or outer set of green leaf-like or highly colored petal-like set of floral parts. Whether they are green or highly colored depends on the flower. The petals are above or inside the sepals. Commonly the petals are showy. But in sugarbowl, globeflower and marsh marigold these conspicuous petals are absent and the sepals become petaloid. They form a companulate "bowl" without any union of parts.

Leaves are pinnately compound with seven to thirteen bimultifid leaflets. They appear to be quite dissected and delicate.

Plants are either erect or climbing. Some grow among the shrubs and use the shrub for stem support. Sugarbowl is found in the open meadows among sage and grasses. At lower elevations they will be in bloom by late June but around 10,000 feet blossoms appear around mid-July.

MEADOWRUE

Thalictrum fendleri   Crowfoot family

It is not the flower of this plant that causes one to be attracted to it, for they are small, greenish, and inconspicuous. The design of the small, dainty leaves makes meadowrue look more like the maidenhair fern or the columbine. It is the abundance of this plant and its delicate leaf and stem structure that causes meadowrue to be classed as one of the common wild flowers in the mountains.

The leaves are divided several times and the individual leaflets appear in series of threes. Each leaflet is palmately veined with toothed edges. There is similarity here with columbine vegetation. These two plants are in the same family.

Male and female flowers arise on different plants. The green minute sepals are present but there are no petals in either male or female flowers. The male flower has numerous pointed stamens and the female flower has several curled-tipped ovaries which, when fertilized, ripen into seeds.

Plants grow in moist areas among aspen groves and among various types of shrubs. They can be grown in home flower gardens. Individuals who cultivate meadowrue find it very useful as "filler" in floral bouquets.

154

Buttercup

Sugarbowl

Meadowrue

CORYDALIS
Golden Smoke and Pink Corydalis

Corydalis aurea
and
Corydalis caseana   Fumitory family

Golden Smoke: Yellow flowers and delicate fern-like leaves growing in low clusters along roadsides in open areas where there is no competition with other vegetation, characterize this species. The flowers of diminutive *C. aurea* are quite unusual. For those who cultivate dutchman's breeches or bleeding heart in their home gardens it is relatively easy to recognize the similar designs of these flowers. There are four petals, the outer two spreading and enclosing the other two which are smaller and united at the tip forming a hood over the stigma (tip of the ovary). One of the outer petals has an enlarged rounded base (a spur).

Pink Corydalis: A delicate, eye-catching, tall cluster (averaging three feet) of pink to light lavender flowers with large two or three pinnately divided fern-like leaves (approximately one foot long). In contrast with the yellow corydalis, which spreads out low and appears on newly disturbed ground, pink corydalis prefers moist and much-shaded areas crowded with many other perennials. The stems are hollow and quite watery. The flower of this species resembles that of golden smoke except in color.

Both golden smoke and pink corydalis deserve more than a casual glance because of the peculiar arrangement of their petals. Delicacy of flower and finely dissected leaf seem to compliment one another.

WALLFLOWER

Erysimum asperum (E. capitatum)   Mustard family

While many mustards bloom early in the summer or even late spring, there are others that prefer mid-July. Some are very selective also in their habitat, but the wallflower pictured here can be found in open pine forest, open meadows, along streams, near spruce and along roadsides. Like the white blooming bittercress, wallflower is one of our mountain's most showy mustards. When the yellow to orange crowded raceme is in full bloom, the flower head is easily seen at some distance.

Reviewing characteristics of mustards (the four crucifer-like separate petals, four small green sepals, six stamens—two at one level and four at the other and a superior ovary) even the amateur can never miss identification of this family.

There is also an alpine wallflower, a different species, but otherwise very similar, that is yellow and yet another species that is rose to purple. The latter is common in the San Juan Mountains.

Golden Smoke (Corydalis)

Pink Corydalis

Wallflower

PENNYCRESS, WILD CANDYTUFT

Thlaspi montanum   Mustard family

This wild flower is not one of the large showy colorful flowers in the mountains for its average height is measured in terms of inches. Rather than compete among the taller perennials and grasses in the rich soil of the open meadows, Pennycress is most often found on thin soil layers over or around exposed rocks and near clusters of dense spruce.

Like many members of the mustard family, this is an early blooming flower, sometimes blooming while snowbanks lie nearby. In mid-June it is the dominant wildflower of the open meadows bursting into blossom before other vegetation has begun to grow.

Flowers are white, blooming in clusters at the tips of leafy stems. Each flower is extremely small with four widely spreading separate petals. The petals appear to form a cross which gives the family its scientific name of Cruciferae. A close look at the stamens reveals a peculiarity of this family—four stamens are at one level (and slightly projecting from the throat) and two stamens are shorter and not evident unless one dissects the floral throat.

The spatulate basal leaves are petioled while the leaves along the stem are more lanceolate and clasp the stalk.

BITTERCRESS

Cardamine cordifolia   Mustard family

This is a relatively tall, densely growing plant with terminal clusters of white flowers. It is found along streams, brooks or seeps. Bittercress loves to have its roots wet. The entire plant may be one to one and a half feet tall where there is sufficient sunlight. Because of the heart-shaped design of the leaf this plant is also known as heartleaf bittercress. The species name given above describes in Latin the heart (cordi) leaf (folia) pattern.

A close inspection of a single flower shows four white petals and six stamens. Four of the stamens are at an equal level and two slightly below. Seed pods are quite distinctive since they may be well formed, erect, and quite elongated (an inch or more long) while upper flowers in the cluster may still be in bloom.

Most detailed features of the Crucifer family have been given with the two flowers previously described.

Pennycress, Wild Candytuft

Bittercress

159

ROCKCRESS

Arabis drummondi   Mustard family

Mustards are typically early blooming types and rockcress is no exception. In the western Colorado mountains one can see rockcress blooming in late June or very early July along open roadsides and meadows. The plant usually grows singularly, is very slender, and may be nearly three feet tall. Flowers are light lavender to pink or white with four petals to each tiny flower. An individual flower could pass unnoticed, as is the case with most mustards, but if there is a sufficient cluster of flowers they can be quite showy.

Leaves along the stem are sessile (without a petiole) and bear a small lobe-like projection at the base. The seed pods are two inches or more long and stand erect along the stem axis. These pods may be quite mature while some flowers are still blooming toward the tip of the axis.

During the latter part of the summer this plant, with its complement of erect pods standing like miniature druids, is conspicuous along road sides.

DRABA
Whitlow-grass or Whitlow-wort

Draba aurea   Mustard family

Colorado West mountains have many wildflowers in the mustard family and all of them are attractive eyecatchers. Some bloom in early summer (many mustards do) and others prefer mid-July. Whitlow-grass is showy during early summer in open rocky meadows at higher elevations (9,000-10,000 feet) and is especially conspicuous in areas such as Flat Tops, Grand Mesa and the San Juans—areas with large natural parklands.

Draba is not a tall plant (averaging about ten cm.) and, to avoid competition with the taller species which thrive in mid-summer, it will have already produced its seedheads before these larger plants bloom. The pods are slightly elongated but flat and often slightly twisted. These fruits will remain for some time on the plant so that if you have missed the blossom the plant is still identifiable by its fruits.

Rockcress

Draba-Whitlow-grass

ROSECROWN and KINGSCROWN

Sedum rosea (Kingscrown)
and
Sedum rhodanthum (Rosecrown)   Orpine family

Rosecrown (Queenscrown) and kingscrown are two of the more unusual wildflowers in our Colorado mountains. Look for these succulent plants with stiff four to ten inch stems in moist open meadows, moist open rocky ground, or in grassy areas along streams from 9,000 to 13,000 feet. Similarities in these two flowers are the smooth fleshy leaves, which arise the full length of the unbranched stem, and the cluster of beautiful blossoms at the tip. In rosecrown this cluster of small flowers is rose-pink with five separate elongated pointed petals and many stamens. Flowers arise from leaf axils along the apex of the stem.

Kingscrown generally is a shorter plant than rosecrown. The flowers are dark red to purple with the five individual petals smaller and more narrow and having protruding stamens. The crowded crown of flowers forms a flat top. After the petals drop, the five ripening ovaries turn the same dark red as the fresh petals so the flower appears to be still in blooom.

Rosecrown terminal blossom clusters are larger and more numerous than the floral head of kingscrown, but the most obvious difference in the two species is the color of the flowers.

Many plants of this family are cultivated in rock gardens around the home.

STONECROP

Sedum lanceolatum   Orpine family

In order to find orpine or yellow stonecrop one must walk through the open meadows and look close to the ground. These open five-pointed star-shaped flowers hug the ground. Stonecrop is also plentiful among rock outcrops where slabs of rock are flush with the ground level. Thus the reason for the name of "stone" crop.

Members of the Orpine family which are common in our Colorado mountains (kingscrown, rose- or queenscrown and stonecrop) are distinguished from the other wildflowers by their thick narrow succulent leaves. These leaves are abundant along the stem axis from floral base to ground level. They are simple lanceolate leaves with an entire margin. In all three of these plants, as the perennial matures in the latter part of the summer, the leaves become tinged with shades of red. Also the enlarged ovaries become reddish. So we not only have a summer floral display but also an autumn show of these striking wildflowers.

Individual stonecrop flowers have five showy, separate, yellow petals and ten delicate projecting stamens. In the center of the flower are five separate but rounded ovaries.

162

Queenscrown

Kingscrown

Stonecrop

SNOWBALL SAXIFRAGE

Saxifraga rhomboidea   Saxifrage family

To look for these small balls of clustered white flowers on top of stout hairy stems (scapes) one must walk along the edges of flowering meadows where there is seep or considerable moisture. The dense flower head arises from a basal rosette of ovate to lanceolate shaped cluster of deep green leaves. Flower heads stand about one foot high so are quite conspicuous among the other native flowers of their particular habitat.

Individual flowers have five white petals separate (not united), ten stamens, and single ovary. All floral parts are well exposed due to the flared nature of the petals.

These flowers are quite abundant in mid-July on moist ground or bog areas at the edge of willow stands or among moisture-loving sedges. Snowball saxifrage is commonly found in association with rose paintbrush, rosecrown and kingscrown. They are never in clusters, rather preferring solitary habit.

There are opinions concerning the origin and meaning of 'saxifraga'. One holds that medieval herbalists used it for a treatment of a disease called 'stones'; and the other idea is that since many grow in crevices they promote the splitting of rocks.

GOOSEBERRY, CURRANT

Ribes wolfii   Saxifrage family

There are two common currant shrubs blooming in mid-summer in the western Colorado mountains. The one pictured here is the more striking of the two shrubs while in bloom. The species of the other shrub is *montigenum* and has small deep rose colored blossoms. Both shrubs may be found in open ground along roadsides, often around large rocks or on poor soil. These currants may be found together, forming a dense mat of shrubs at the edge of spruce or aspen stands.

The one pictured here has greenish white sepals and petals (the sepals are larger and more showy than the petals). A black berry is produced in fruit. There are no spines in this species but *montigenum* does have spines and stiff bristles. The fruit of *R. montigenum* is red and that of *R. wolfii* is black.

Leaves of these plants are quite distinctive with their palmately veined and palmately lobed pattern.

Many people are familiar with the cultivated currants and gooseberries. Some of the wild species are also edible.

The saxifrage family is a widely divergent group. Besides the cultivated and wild gooseberries and currants, it includes mock orange, coralbells, fendlerbrush and grass of parnassus.

Snowball Saxifrage

Gooseberry, Currant

POTENTILLA

Potentilla fruticosa (Pentaphylloides floribunda)
       and
Potentilla pulcherrima   Rose family

Potentilla is also called cinquefoil because of the five leaflets comprising a single leaf evident in some species. "Cinque" means five in French and "foil" is an old English word for leaf. Flowers are bright yellow or lemon yellow and could be mistaken for buttercups. However, potentilla has a cup-shaped base (hypanthium) from which the five yellow petals and usually twenty stamens arise. Also, the yellow of the petal is not as waxy looking as that of the buttercup flower.

Several species of potentilla are common in the Colorado mountains; consequently, it is hard to pick just one or two for display here. One selected and shown is a much branched shrub (*P. fruticosa*) averaging one to four feet tall, mostly in open places; and the other, also a perennial (*P. pulcherrima*), but slender stemmed (an herbaceous plant) with flowers borne in loose, open clusters. The latter species averages about two feet in height.

P. fruticosa is one of the best performing shrubs in the mountains. It is very hardy, produces much shrubbery and exhibits bright yellow flowers all summer. It can be easily grown at lower elevations in our State as a decorative home garden ornamental. Nurseries carry these shrubs in their sale stock.

In heavily grazed high mountain meadows *P. pulcherrima* and others of the potentillas are abundant because cattle find them unpalatable.

Some of the other bright yellow blooming herbs in our mountains are *P. arguta*, *P. gracilis*, *P. pennsylvanica* and *P. concinna*.

ROSE

Rosa woodsii   Rose family

"A rose is a rose is a rose," said Gertrude Stein and there isn't an individual around who wouldn't agree with this poetic statement. Roses are easily recognized because they are so similar to some of our cultivated types. The five petaled pink or rose-red blossoms surround the numerous yellow stamens. Occasionally one can find bushes of white blossomed roses in the mountains. Petals and stamens line the urn-shaped hypanthium (tube) in which are located the seeds (achenes). At maturity this urn-shaped tube becomes fleshy and develops into the fruit.

The dark red "fruit" (called rose-hips) is round, smooth, and averages slightly less than a half inch across when mature. These hips provide winter food for the mountain wildlife. They have also been important in the diet of the Indians and early settlers because they are rich in vitamin C. Rose hips may be gathered and made into jelly or tea.

The famous rose fragrance is also present in the wild rose.

166

**Potentilla
fruticosa**

**Potentilla
pulcherrina**

Rose

THIMBLEBERRY and RASPBERRY

Rubus parviflorus (Thimbleberry)
      and
Rubus idaeus (Raspberry)   erry)   Rose family

Thimbleberry is a low perennial shrub often in dense stands among firs and aspen. It prefers rocky slopes where soil is thin or lacking. The similarity between raspberries and roses is more than superficial for thimbleberry belongs to the same genus as raspberry and all three belong to the rose family. Compare the pictures of raspberry and thimbleberry. The woody stems, however, are without bristles or prickles and the leaves are simple. Mature leaves of thimbleberry may be over five inches across, show palmate venation, and are divided into five triangular pointed lobes with serrated edge. These leaves are quite distinctive of the plant. When both leaves and flowers are present there is no question as to identity.

Flowers are large (sometimes more than an inch across) with five white petals and innumerable stamens. In the fall a red berry forms as an edible fruit, although it is not nearly as savory as the fruit of raspberry.

Thimbleberry prefers moist shaded slopes with a thin layer of rich soil and raspberry prefers dry sunny talus slopes or areas of poor soil. Raspberry is commonly found along roadsides.

PINK PLUMES

Geum triflorum (Erythrocoma triflora)   Rose family

Also called Long-plumed Avens, here is a real jewel of delicate beauty. So dainty and small are these pink pendant lamp-posts that they will be missed unless one leaves the roadway and leisurely strolls through the open meadows. Not only does the entire nodding flower show a delicate shade of rose-pink but also the floral stem and the feathery plumes of the seeds are lightly tinted with pink.

The five tiny pointed spurs are bractlets which alternate with the five sepals and petals. This combination of sepals, petals and bractlets encloses and conceals the many stamens.

The fern-like leaves are mostly basal and finely dissected. The few stem leaves are much reduced.

When pink plumes goes to seed in mid-August the light pink feathery plumes produced appear like powder-puffs. Few wildflowers put on two shows, one as a flower and one in fruit.

Thimbleberry

Raspberry

Pink Plumes

STRAWBERRY

Fragaria virginiana (F. ovalis)   Rose family

Here is a wild flower that really needs no special introduction. If one doesn't recognize the trifoliate serrated leaflets or the white, broadly rounded, five petaled flowers with many yellow stamens and ovaries, then surely the strawberry's red and juicy fruit is well known to us.

The fruits are small as compared to our cultivated varieties but sweet and delicious just the same. They generally begin to ripen in early August.

Strawberries spread by aerial runners (stolons) so that one often finds them in clustered groups (the well known strawberry patch). They love the dark rich acid loam of the mountains and therefore, are quite common. They are small plants, hugging the ground so they are not seen unless one parts the grass or other perennials and looks closely.

Many members of the rose family are of great importance to man. A goodly number of them have been cultivated for food and ornamentals. And some hardy individuals enjoy late summer visits to the mountains gathering chokecherries, raspberries, serviceberries and strawberries, all members of the same family.

SERVICEBERRY

Amelanchier alnifolia   Rose family

Serviceberry is a moderately tall shrub growing in rocky soil along the flanks of our mountains of Colorado West in a wide zone from oakbrush to aspen. It is most common in the scrub oak zone where it is associated with mountain mahogany, sage and chokecherry. The white flowers are produced in clusters, each flower having five elongated strap-like petals, arising from the rim of a green cup (the calyx tube). Stamens are numerous and, like the petals, arise from the rim of this tube.

The fruit of this shrub is purplish-black when ripe and, though edible, is rather bitter to the taste. It is classed as a pome, botanically speaking, which is the same type of fruit as the apple. Birds and other forms of wildlife usually eat them before man has a chance to collect.

Leaves are simple, quite rounded, and with coarsely toothed margins. They are lighter colored and somewhat hairy along the veins on the underside.

This is truly a beautiful flowering shrub during the early summer. There is a horticulturalized variety that one may purchase and plant in the lawn.

CHOKECHERRY

Prunus virginiana   Rose family

A tall shrub common along the roadsides and along streams in the oakbrush zone. Chokecherry prefers the 7000-9000 foot elevation which includes much of the lower mountainous region of western Colorado. It is usually associated with serviceberry and mountain mahogany in these areas.

Flowers are white and fragrant and are borne in a raceme. They are very much like the flower of a cherry or plum because these plants are of the same genus. Other cultivated types such as peach, apricot or almond are of the same genus. Small wonder that this wild type would produce an edible fruit. Close inspection of an individual flower shows fine spreading petals and many stamens. Leaves average three to four inches long and are finely serrate.

Many people enjoy gathering chokecherries the latter part of the summer and making them into jams and jellies. The small reddish-purple fruit is similar to a cherry with a fleshy pulp surrounding a single seed. When eaten fresh the fruit produces a puckering of the mouth and throat, giving rise to the term chokecherry or chokeberry.

Strawberry

Serviceberry

Chokecherry

LUPINE

Lupinus argenteus   Pea family

Lupines have pea-like flowers, commonly blue or purple, and borne usually in long, showy, spike-like clusters (racemes). They are one of the most common wildflowers along the flanks of our mountains from the oakbrush zone to areas near timberline. The top petal is called the banner, the two side petals are the wings and the pointed incurved keel comprises the lower two pointed petals. Stamens are united into a tube which surrounds the pistil. The fruit is a pod (legume) with several seeds. Leaves are composed of four to seventeen leaflets (palmately compound) which aid in distinguishing the blooming lupine from the blue-flowered spike-like clusters of the penstemons. These two wildflowers, penstemon and lupine, may be found blooming together along road cuts and open areas flanking the sides of the mountains.

One of the more common lupines at higher elevations (and the one pictured) averages two to three feet tall in bloom. Large conspicuous clumps of this lupine are common along road cuts and in open meadow areas. They are in full bloom during July. Occasionally one may see a pink variety blooming amid a mass of the blues.

Reports indicate the seeds and pods are poisonous to livestock.

Many gardeners recognize lupine because it is easily cultivated. The famous Texas bluebonnet is the same genus.

VETCHES and PEAVINES

Lathyrus leucanthus (white peavine)
and
Vicia americana (vetch)   Pea family

In mid-summer one can often spread apart a mass of vegetation in the mountains and find, upon close inspection, white to yellowish or purple to pink flowers characteristic of the pea family. Peavine, as the name would indicate, is a small-stemmed trailing vine winding itself through the vegetation in open shaded areas of the forest. Because of its weak stem, both peavine and vetch use other plants as their support.

The flower has the characteristic banner (upper petal) wings(a petal on either side as it faces you), and the keel (two petals united into a boat-like keel). These floral features are characteristic of our garden pea or bean flower. These flowers also form a pod in fruit.

Leaves also are similar to those of a garden pea with two to several pairs of leaflets and a terminal hair-like tendril. These two to several pairs of leaflets and tendril form a single leaf (pinnately compound leaf).

There are structural differences between peavines and vetches. Vetches (*Vicia*) generally have smaller leaflets and flowers and there is a tuft of hairs at the tip of the style; whereas, in peavines (*Lathyrus*) the leaf segments and flowers are generally larger and the tuft of hair is along the upper side of the style.

Lupine

White Sweetpea

Vetch

GOLDENBANNER, GOLDENPEA

Thermopsis montana Pea family

This bright yellow flower, which adds color to the mid-summer display of wildflowers, is also called false lupine. There are two distinct features of this flower and plant that make it easy to recognize. During flowering, the most conspicuous feature is the blossom which has the typical pattern of many of the common members of the pea family. Like the sweet pea grown in our gardens it has a large upper flared petal called the banner, two side petals forming the wings and two lower, united petals forming a projecting keel.

The other distinctive feature of goldenbanner is the tri-foliate arrangement of the leaflets (palmately compound). This is common among members of the pea family, especially the clovers.

Seed pods are also typically pea family. With all of these characteristics one is able to see much similarity with another very common wildflower of this same pea family, the blue lupine. It is understandable, therefore, that false lupine is another name for this plant.

Goldenbanner enjoys both full sun of the open meadow and partial shade of the evergreens. Large clumps of this flower are very common all through the Montane and Subalpine areas of our State.

FLAX

Linum lewisii Flax family

Flax flowers could easily be the baisc, typical or model flower for any beginner to study. It has five separate sepals, all green, and five separate showy petals, all colored. Stamens are five in number also, showing very well the parts of filament and anther (pollen bearing unit). In the center of the flower is the conspicuous ovary which is superior (stands above the sepals and petals), and is composed of five united carpels. This floral pattern of flax is standard to any botany teacher or student.

Flax is common at lower elevations in late May and, as spring progresses up the flanks of the mountains, one can find it blooming all the way up into the Subalpine zone. It is especially prevalent in open meadows around 10,000 feet.

Flax has been important to man's well-being for many years because some members of the family produce a very tough fiber. The old world flax is well known for its linen thread and the American Indian used prairie flax for the same purpose.

GERANIUM

Geranium richardsonii Geranium family

One of the few instances among our native wildflowers where the common name and generic name are the same. However, the wild species varies in leaf design and numbers of flowers in a cluster from the potted geranium (genus *Pelargonium*) we know in our home and flower borders.

Geraniums are widely distributed in the mountains blooming during mid-summer and continuing to bloom through most of July. In an early summer they may even appear in bloom in late June, especially at lower elevations. They are relatively easy to recognize with their palmately-veined, five-lobed deep green leaves. Most leaves arise from the basal rootstock and are long stemmed but some are borne along the stem. The flowers are white to rose-lavender with the veins showing distinct darker shades, as though they had been beautifully and carefully outlined with a colored pencil. The flower has five distinct showy petals and ten projecting stamens. Geraniums are most common in open grassy meadows, most often with one or two stalks to a cluster. Some of the older unmolested perennial plants form clusters nearly a foot in diameter.

Goldenbanner

Flax

Geranium

CHECKERMALLOW

Sidalcea neomexicana   Hollyhock family

Also called New Mexico checkermallow and wild hollyhock, this mountain cousin of our common garden hollyhock is not difficult to find in Colorado. In open wet meadows of North Park, Middle Park, upper Yampa River and Gunnison Basin during mid-July it will be one of the dominant showy flowering species. They are easily seen from the auto because they are taller than the grasses among which they grow; the pink flowering stalks show well above the grass tops.

Flowers are an inch or more across, arise in racemes along the upper axes and are a very showy medium pink. The entire stalk may be three to four feet tall. An individual flower has five large pink petals, each over one half inch long. In the center is the projected column of anthers. The many anthers and stigmas are crowded together to form this column. Filaments of the stamens are fused into a cylinder which surrounds the fused styles. The ovary is superior (stands above the receptacle) but cannot be seen because the fused filaments surround it.

Upper leaves are very much maple-like with five to seven deeply toothed lobes; whereas, the basal leaves are only slightly lobed, resembling those of a geranium.

WILD HOLLYHOCK

Iliamna rivularis   Mallow family

Our common garden hollyhock is so familiar to us that this mountain "cousin" is not difficult to find. Wild or Mountain hollyhock is especially common in the central and northern mountain areas. Look for these large flowered, single stalked plants in moist areas along streams and in open meadows. Occasionally the petals are shades of pink to lavender.

Flowers are an inch or more across, arise in racemes along the upper axes and are very showy. The entire stalk may be three to four feet tall. An individual flower has five large white petals, each over one-half inch long. In the center is the projecting column of anthers. The many anthers and stigmas are crowded together to form this column. Filaments of the stamens are fused into a cylinder which surrounds the fused styles. The ovary is superior (stands above the receptacle) but is not able to be seen because the fused filaments surround it.

Leaves are very much maple-like with five to seven deeply toothed lobes with some pubescence.

Checkermallow

Wild Hollyhock

VIOLET

Viola adunca (purple)
and
Viola nuttallii (yellow)

Violet family

There are a few flowers in the continental United States that are native to most every state; and therefore, a flower easily recognized by the amateur. The violet is one of these which is common in moist woodlands and forested areas from coast to coast. There are several states which have adopted the violet as their state flower.

In the higher mountains of our State violets occur in the typical woodland habitat. Since these are low growing plants, four to five inches tall, and sheltered under spruce or occasionally in open meadows crowded by taller more conspicuous plants, one must look closely to find them. Blossoms may be slight variations of violet or blue or may be yellow to white. Large, broad, oval leaves often grow taller than the flowers and make them less conspicuous.

Flowers are usually solitary, arising from the base of the plant. There are five petals, the lowest one having a spur or deep sac at the base.

Violets are difficult to identify because they hybridize freely in nature. Also, many types will produce flowers that do not open; thus insuring self-fertilization and seeds for future generations.

FIREWEED

Epilobium angustifolium

Evening Primrose family

This hardly seems an appropriate name for so stately and beautiful a flower. The name fireweed refers to the fact that it is one of the first plants to invade barren land after a fire. It grows very well in newly disturbed ground along roadside cuts. We are fortunate to have such a showy and beautiful flower to heal the scars made by man. Flowers are a penetrating magenta to deep rose pink which bloom from mid-July to late August. Flowers start to appear from the basal portion of the inflorescence and gradually mature upward along the stalk. In later stages of growth, flowers may be in full bloom; while below, pod-like capsules are quite mature with contained seeds.

An individual flower has four petals and eight protruding stamens. Sepals, petals and stamens arise above the ovary and in this instance the term inferior ovary is used. This is typical of all members of the Evening Primrose family.

Leaves are long and narrow with an entire margin. Veins in the leaf are united along the margin producing a scalloped effect.

Fireweed is a late summer prominent roadside flower in all of western Colorado at higher elevations. You will not miss it because plants can be three feet tall in favorable locations.

Purple Violet

Yellow Violet

Fireweed

MOUNTAIN PARSLEY

Pseudocymopterus montanus   Carrot or Parsnip family

Mountain Parsley is a prolific plant in open meadows in all of the western Colorado mountains but not particularly striking to the observer until one walks slowly across the open meadow. These flat-topped clusters of small yellow flowers produced at the top of the stem grow from four to eight inches tall. An occasional wild yellow parsley will grow to a foot in height if not in crowded conditions and where soil and moisture are favorable. Other flowers of the open meadow are usually taller than mountain parsley. This type of inflorescence, typical of members of the carrot family in which all pedicels arise from the same point and form a symmetrical flat top, is called an umbel.

Leaves on most members of this family are also quite similar, resembling the finely dissected pattern that we know in carrots and parsley. Also at the base of the leaf there is a characteristic clasping sheath.

Mountain parsley is abundant in western Colorado mountains in July. It is one of the dominant wildflowers on the open meadows of the Subalpine zone.

COW PARSNIP

Heracleum lanatum   Carrot or parsnip family

Few plants are more appropriately named than is cow parsnip. Not only does it have parsnip-like leaves and the same type of inflorescence and seeds (they are in the same family), but also the plant is truly cowsize. This plant when in bloom can easily stand four to five feet tall. To find this flower, which blooms from mid-July to first part of August in our mountains, one looks among moist aspen groves. The large flattopped flower cluster is white and very showy. It averages six to eight inches across. Usually the stalks stand above most other vegatation crowding around them. The generic name *Heracleum* refers to Hercules, implying size of plant.

A closer inspection of the inflorescence reveals the characteristic pattern for all members of the carrot family. It is a compound umbel; that is, the individual flowers arise at the tips of clustered rays which in turn arise from the tips of larger rays. It is rather like an umbrella with small secondary umbrellas arising from the tips of the larger umbrella spokes.

Leaves are divided into three large leaflets, each leaflet palmately veined with irregular toothed and notched margins.

Mountain Parsley

Cow Parsnip

LOVEROOT

Ligusticum porteri   Carrot or Parsnip family

Also called lovage, wild celery or wild parsnip, this is a tall stout perennial with white blossoms and fern-like leaves. Flower clusters are born in compound umbels, typical of the carrot family. In this type of inflorescence many short stalks which arise at a common point on the stem in turn give rise to a series of rays from which the flowers arise. The pattern of the inflorescence in this family is much more characteristic than is the detail of a single tiny flower. Another characteristic of many members of this family is the carrot-like pattern of the leaves which are large, finely dissected and mostly basal.

Its leaves have been used in place of celery for seasoning soups, since these two plants have similarities of foliage.

Loveroot has aromatic roots with a distinctive fragrance. It has been used in the treatment of coughs, colds, upset stomach and even the common headache. A very good plant to have close by!

The parsnip family has several other plants which produce flavoring. Some of these are parsley, dill and caraway. Some vegetables of the family are carrot, parsnip and celery.

In mid-July Lovage is a dominant flower of open meadows in the Subalpine zone, since it stands a foot or more above the other flowers of the area.

COLORADO DOGWOOD

Cornus stolonifera   Dogwood family

Most individuals think of the large white or pink flowered shrubs native of the southeastern United States when they see the name dogwood. The four large petaloid bracts that make the southeastern dogwood so showy are not present in our Colorado dogwood so the flower is smaller and less conspicuous. An individual flower has four small white petals and four stamens. Sepals are present but very inconspicuous.

Many small white flowers produce a flat-topped cyme. The entire inflorescence when in full bloom is slightly more than an inch across. Our dogwood is a low shrub found at the edge of aspen groves or among rocky outcrops and along roadsides. They bloom in mid-July and produce a whitish drupe (a cherry-like fruit) after the flower has bloomed. Associated plants include chokecherry, raspberry and serviceberry.

Other characteristic features of the Colorado dogwood are the opposite simple leaves with entire margins and a wine colored twig, especially obvious in young twigs in early spring before the leaves come out.

Loveroot

Colorado Dogwood

183

KINNIKINNIK
(Bearberry)

Arctostaphylos uva-ursi   Heath family

Manzanitas are common shrubs on the lower slopes of the Sierra Nevada Range of California and we generally consider them as part of the chapparal of the western United States. But bearberry is one of the manzanitas which grows in Colorado as a low, prostrate, trailing evergreen shrub covering the forest floor in partial shade of the spruce forests. Extensive vegetative ground cover may be so abundant as to exclude other shrubs or herbaceous plants. Other conditions under which bearberry grows is the well drained, rocky or gravelly soil within the Montane and Subalpine zones. The habit of forming a dense ground cover makes the species valuable for watershed protection.

Flowers occur in May or June, depending on the elevation. They are not showy; rather one must lift the leafy stems where the dainty pink cluster of inverted urn-shaped flowers are located. The flowers give way in the late summer to round deep pink to red, smooth berries. These berries are eaten by bear and other wildlife; thus the common name of bearberry. The species name of *uva-ursi* translated loosely says bear's berry.

The word kinnikinnick is an Algonquian Indian word which referred to a mixture of dried leaves and bark used for tobacco.

SHOOTING STAR

Dodecatheon pulchellum   Primrose family

Imagine a flower riding through space at thousands of miles per hour and you have a good mental image of all species of shooting stars. The five rose-lavender petals are curved sharply backward and the five stamens form a brown-black projectile point out and beyond the reflexed petals. No other wildflower is so appropriately named. There is a continuous yellow wavy line at the base of the five petals in many of the species. With such distinction, one need not describe the details of an individual flower.

The two species in our State prefer moist shaded areas along small streams or growing in seeps at elevations of approximately 6,000 to 10,000 feet. At their lower range they will be blooming by late May and along the small streams near the base of Loveland Pass flowering time is mid-July. If it is a dry spring and summer they will not bloom.

All leaves are linear to lanceolate and form a basal rosette. This is a vegetative characteristic of many primroses.

PRIMROSE

Primula parryi   Primrose family

Alpine primrose is not as common in the mountains as many of the others reported here. However, since it is such a beautiful and striking flower, it has been included. One finds alpine or Parry primrose along small streams or moist areas. At lower elevations it needs some degree of shade, but above timberline where alpine primrose is most common, it can be found in the wet areas along the rivulets and streams among the short tundra grasses. Blossom time is mid- to late July, depending on the area.

The plants average six to eight inches in height with the stalk capped by a cluster of eight to twelve flowers. It is the flower cluster, which appears in late July, that gives the Parry primrose its striking beauty. The flowers are dark purplish-red with a yellow dotted centers. An individual flower has five funnel-shaped fused petals which open into five spreading separate lobes. The flowers are quite foul smelling, contrary to what one would think when observing their beauty.

All leaves arise from a basal rosette and are quite elongate-spatulate in outline.

Kinnikinnik (Bearberry)

Shooting Star

Primrose

GREEN GENTIAN

Frasera speciosa [*Swertia radiata*]   Gentian family

Occasionally there is a plant that seems totally different from the others and could be recognized in its natural habitat after a brief study of its picture. Green gentian, also called monument plant, is just such a conspicuous plant. It is aptly named monument plant because it stands three to four feet tall in the rich soil of open meadows and is taller than all other plants in its environment. In areas where grazing is heavy, these plants are shorter and possibly more numerous. These gentians may form dense stands in some areas of the White River Plateau (Flattops), but become less common as one travels southward in the State. From a distance it can be confused with false hellebore which also produces a towering solitary spike-like inflorescence.

The pale green leaves are arranged in whorls of three to seven. They are large and broad at the base but become gradually reduced to bracts at the top. Several flowers may arise at each bract so that many flowers may be open along the upper portion of the stem. Color in flowers is greenish-white dotted with purple. The four slender sepals alternate with the four wider light green star-shaped petals. Two fringed glands are present at the base of each petal.

FRINGED GENTIAN

Gentianopsis thermalis (*Gentiana thermalis*)   Gentian family

Fringed gentian is of the same family as green gentian. This gentian rates a distinctive name because it has a fringe along the edge of the petal lobes. This jagged edging is more pronounced in the sinuses between the petal lobes and lessens toward the tip. However, there is variation among the flowers in the degree of fringing of the petals.

ʻ Like many gentian species, fringed gentian is also an annual plant and blooms in early August. Rose gentian and fringed gentian are often found together in open meadows of the Subalpine zone. The flowers of fringed gentian are considerably larger than the other blue gentians. They may be from one to two inches tall. The flowers open during the day and close toward evening. Only the lobes of the petals open, the lower part of the petals are united into a slender tube.

The sepals may be tinted with blue, particularly along their fused margins.

Gentians have frequently been the subject of poems and legends.

Green Gentian

Fringed Gentian

JACOBS-LADDER

Polemonium pulcherrimum ssp. *delicatum*   Phlox family

Jacobs-ladder or skunkleaf are two names for this wildflower which are quite descriptive of parts or odor of the plant. Jacobs-ladder is so named from the ladder-like arrangement of the leaflets, and skunkleaf is derived from the skunk-like odor of the crushed leaf. Since the name skunkleaf is also used for leafy polemonium, in order to avoid confusion, perhaps this title should not be favored over Jacobs-Ladder.

This low plant blooms in mid-July and is common under open stands of spruce where there is reduced sunlight. Delicate light blue bell-shaped flowers with five somewhat excluded stamens are produced on slender stalks in open clusters. The leaves, with their ladder-like arrangement, are sometimes mistaken for fern leaves.

Jacobs-ladder may be easily differentiated from leafy polemonium in two ways. First, the height of the plant. Jacobs-ladder is usually no more than six to eight inches tall; whereas, leafy polemonium is generally two to three feet in height. Second, the leaves (not leaflets) are predominantly basal in Jacobs-ladder and in leafy polemonium the leaves arise along the stem.

LEAFY POLEMONIUM

Polemonium foliosissimum   Phlox family

Sometimes called skunkleaf due to the skunk odor produced from crushed leaves or pressed specimens. Since the name skunkleaf is used also for Jacobs-ladder, perhaps the term leafy polemonium should be used for this plant.

Leafy polemonium may be easily differentiated from Jacobs-ladder by two plant qualities. Leafy polemonium, while in bloom, stands two to three feet tall; whereas, Jacobs-ladder is quite diminutive, ranging from six to eight inches. The leaves of leafy polemonium arise along the stem while in Jacobs-ladder they are predominantly basal.

Leafy polemonium is usually found in tall, erect clumps in open meadows and road cuts, preferably in the upper Montane zone. They enjoy full sunlight as compared to Jacobs-ladder which prefers dense shade of the spruce. Like Jacobs-ladder, the flowers are borne in open clusters.

Other dark blue flowers growing in clusters along road cuts which might be confused with leafy polemonium without close inspection are phacelia and the two common species of penstemon. All of these mentioned flowers are products of early summer.

Jacobs-Ladder

Leafy Polemonium

SCARLET GILIA and PINK GILIA

Ipomopsis aggregata ssp. *formosissima*
and
Ipomopsis aggregata ssp. *attenuata*   Phlox family

If the columbine is the emblem of the state of Colorado, scarlet gilia could well be the floral insignia for Colorado West. Sometimes they are so profuse that they may be the dominant flower on an entire meadow about mid-July. Scarlet gilia, skyrocket gilia or fairy trumpet are all proper names describing this showy, scarlet trumpet.

Plants stand twelve to fifteen inches tall with pinnately divided fine fern-like leaves. The delicacy of the leaves seems to fit the dainty fairy trumpet.

An individual trumpet (corolla) may be over an inch long with pointed spreading lobes at the tip. Five stamens project slightly from the throat. Some plants have widely separated trumpets but others have most of these flowers grouped in a terminal cluster.

These are hardy plants with woody taproots. Besides growing in dry exposd open meadows, scarlet gilia is common along road cuts and scattered under open stands of spruce and fir. They do best in sunny locations and on dry ground.

Scarlet gilia is truly one of nature's finest creations. The name gilia is spanish (named from an 18th century Spanish botanist).

Pink gilia is one of the dominant flowers in open meadows in the high plateaus, such as Flat Tops, Grand Mesa, Uncompahgre uplift and Battlement Mesa. Greatest profusion of bloom is latter part of July.

190

Scarlet Gilia

Pink Gilia

191

WATERLEAF

Hydrophyllum fendleri (Fendler waterleaf)
and
Hydrophyllum capitatum (low waterleaf)   Waterleaf family

The name "waterleaf" is the translation of the genus name *Hydrophyllum* (hydro - water and phyllum - leaf). Some tropical members of this family have pockets of water in the leaves and this quality has given rise to the Latin name for the group.

Floral characteristics of plants are the same except for color of petals. In Fendler waterleaf they are white, pink to violet; whereas, in low waterleaf they are light to deep blue. Both are in dense terminal clusters which are longer than the subtending leaves (*H. fendleri*) or shorter than the subtending leaves (*H. capitatum*). The five petals are united into a bell-shaped corolla with five stamens protruding from the flower center like pins from a pincushion. This adds to the beauty of the flower cluster. Leaves are divided into toothed leaflets (usually 5-13 main divisions per leaf, depending on species).

Fendler waterleaf blooms mid-summer, usually on well drained soil. It may be found among broken rock outcrops (where there is enough soil for them to be established) and next to spruce—dry ground but somewhat shaded. Low waterleaf needs deep rich soil, mostly open grassy meadows although it can be found among oak brush in late May. Neither of these waterleafs are particular about elevation; both are in Montane and Subalpine zones.

PHACELIA

Phacelia sericea   Waterleaf family

There are several common names given to members of this genus because they vary enough to be quite distinctive. Some are called scorpionweed because the inflorescence is coiled with flowers borne in two rows along the stem. The curled flower cluster supposedly resembles the arched tail of a scorpion. This type is typical of the desert species. Others have the flowers crowded into rather dense spike-like panicles. Some have very pronounced exerted stamens and are called purple fringe or purple pincushion; while others do not have the projected stamens. The entire genus is a difficult one to work with because some of the species may actually be varieties of a single species.

Other common names for purple pincushion are wild heliotrope and purple fringe.

The phlox-like flowers of phacelia have five exerted stamens which are about twice as long as the petals. It is the prominence of these stamens that gives rise to the name purple fringe of purple pincushion. Phacelia is a beautiful plant with a single clump bearing as many as eight or twelve stalks averaging two feet tall. They prefer non-crowded conditions, commonly seen along road cuts, but occasionally found in open meadows from June to August.

Scorpionweed is discussed in the desert wildflower section of this book.

Waterleaf capitatum

Waterleaf fendlerii

Phacelia

GIANT HYSSOP

Agastache urticifolia   Mint family

Giant hyssop of horsemint may be as much as four to five feet tall, especially when grown in rich moist soil under the shade of aspen. It is a coarse-looking plant partially because of its open branching system and partially because of the hairiness of the stems and leaves. At the tip of each branch is a two to four inch spike of closely compacted faint pink to lavender flowers, each subtended by a small leaf-like bract.

Flowers are typically mint in pattern. A united corolla (collective term for petals) with a bilabiate or two-lipped pattern of the lobes. The two upper lobes of the corolla are erect and the three lower lobes are spreading. Four functional stamens protrude from the throat of the corolla.

Stems are square which is also a mint family characteristic. Leaves are opposite and ovate with toothed margins.

Giant hyssop is often found in clumps because the plants have a large rootstock and spread easily by this means. An individual plant could easily be bypassed for it takes more than one or two flower heads to make any kind of coloration among the various shades of greenery of the landscape. It is most common near the oakbrush-aspen contact where it can be found blossoming from June through August.

BEEBALM

Monarda fistulosa   Mint family

The beebalms are recognized as members of the mint family by their four angled stems, opposite leaves and the fruits, which consist of four small nutlets, included within the persistent outer flower parts (calyx). Flowers of our common species in the western Colorado mountains are a brightly colored rose-lavender to lavender-purple, large and showy and borne in a dense terminal cluster surrounded by leafy bracts. Among open meadows and along roadsides beebalm will be obvious when in bloom because it stands about 12-13 inches tall and, therefore, above the native grasses with which it is associated.

Flowers are strongly two-lipped with only two anther bearing, usually exerted stamens. The elongated calyx has five nearly equal teeth and is hairy externally.

Some species of monarda are grown in our gardens, others have the volatile oil thymol which is a valuable antiseptic drug. The leaves have a taste strongly suggestive of sage(*Salvia*) but that would be understandable since both monarda and salvia are in the same family.

Other common names for this species are bergamot and horsemint (although this name is usually associated with *Agastache*).

Giant Hyssop

Beebalm

MERTENSIA, BLUEBELLS

Mertensia franciscana   Borage family

This is an instance in which the scientific name is used almost as often as the common name. Mertensia is easily recognized with its many blue bell-shaped, pendant flowers on one to three foot stems. The pink color commonly observed in the flower cluster is usually due to unopened blossoms; but occasionally flowers on a plant are pink, even when in full bloom. Clusters of the bells arise on pendant slender stems from the several nodes of the upper portion of the flowering stalk. The weight of the flowers is sufficient to cause the entire flowering stalk to nod.

A single bell (flower) is composed of five united petals forming a bell-shaped tube. The five scalloped edges of the petals are evident at the outer edge of the bell.

Bluebells may occur in large clusters as much as three feet tall along roadsides where competition with other plants is at a minimum. Or they may be found in rich dark soil under shaded aspen and spruce or mingled with undershrubs.

The leaves are quite distinctive with their smooth entire margin and prominent veins. There are other mertensias in the Rocky Mountains that do not have these distinct lateral veins.

DUSKY PENSTEMON

Penstemon whippleanus   Figwort family

This is one of the large group of flowers which are called beardstongue. There are many species in the mountains, and several showy forms of penstemon (also often used as a common name) are common on the upper slopes of Montane zone in western Colorado mountains. The hairs at the tip of the fifth (sterile) stamen give it the name of beardstongue. Whipplean or dusky penstemon is different than most flowers in that this same species has both the wine-purple to almost black-purple color flower on some plants and other plants bear a dull white to light cream color flower. The white variety is most common on the high plateaus of the mountainous western edge of our State.

Dusky penstemon is very hardy, most often found encroaching among the gravels along the roadside. They are probably one of the more common flowers along the roadbed.

The plant when in flower averages ten to twelve inches high with the flower clustered toward the top. An individual flower has petals united into a narrow elongated tube with the outer lobes spreading into the typical two-lipped design of the figwort family.

Mertensia, Bluebells

Dusky Penstemon

PENSTEMON

Penstemon strictus
Penstemon mensarum
Penstemon rydbergii   Figwort family

Known also as beardstongues because of the hairs at the tip of the fifth (sterile) stamen in most of the species. This hairy, sterile stamen projects into the throat of the flower. The showy light blue or dark blue (or more rarely, cream-white or red, depending on the species) flowers cover the many erect stems, which are sometimes one to three feet tall. The individual flower is strongly two-lipped (like the snapdragon flower) with four functional stamens and one sterile staminode in our plants. They may be confused with lupine at a distance because of the color and arrangement of individual flowers along the stem, but the two-lip arrangement of the petals and elongated lance-shaped leaves differentiate it from the lupine.

Penstemons are very common in the mountainous and desert areas of western Colorado. They frequently form large patches of solid blue in favored locales. Two very common species, *P. structus* and *P. mensarum* occur along road cuts within the Montane zone. Their flowers may be shades of dark blue and pink or rarely white. *P. strictus* occurs lower in altitude than *P. mensarum*. *P. rydbergii*, on the other hand, is found only in open meadows at altitudes of around 10,000 feet. It is easy to differentiate from other western Colorado penstemons because the inflorescence is crowded in a terminal head rather than racemes with flowers arising along the axis. Also, the flower color is darker blue-lavender with a shade of pink.

Penstemon strictus

Penstemon mensarum

Penstemon rydbergii

PAINTBRUSH

Castilleja rhexifolia (rose)
Castilleja miniata (orange-red)
Castilleja sulphurea (yellow)   Figwort family

Paintbrush, painted cup of Indian paint brush is the state flower of Wyoming, and an abundant flower of western Colorado open meadows and wooded areas. They occur from the lower elevations of our State to above timberline in a wide variety of vegetative types. Three common species shown here may be recognized by color—a light yellow, a fire red, and deep rose. Variations of these species may be white, light rose and orange shades. The strange feature of this flower is that its beautiful color is not the flower, but a result of the numerous brightly colored bracts (modified leaves) crowded at the tip of the "flower". The small and inconspicuous flower is hidden within the colored bracts.

The green petals are strongly two-lipped and enclose the four stamens, which are arranged in two pairs of unequal length. Paintbrushes are in the same family as the common snapdragon with its two-lipped petals, the design of the two-lips can be seen with the upper lip entire and elongated and the lower lip very short and three toothed. When the flower is mature, the corolla appears projected out from its surrounding colored bracts like elongated green horns.

The dark green leaves are narrow and entire or dissected into narrow lobes and vary from nearly hairless to somewhat woolly-hairy. Stems are usually tufted and either branched or unbranched.

Yellow and red varieties of paintbrush are most common along the upper slopes and open meadows; whereas, the rose variety is restricted to more boggy areas of open meadows. Some of the nicer clumps in mid-summer will be in the Subalpine zone.

200

Rose Paintbrush

Orange Paintbrush

Yellow Paintbrush

MONKEYFLOWER

Mimulus guttatus   Figwort family

One looks for monkeyflower growing along seeps, springs, or edges of small brooks. They will grow even in standing water. The stems are weak and in their decumbent position cause rooting at the stem joints (nodes). This tends to form a solid mat or clump of monkeyflower. They are common in upper Montane and Subalpine wet areas from June to September.

Flowers are bright yellow often with reddish-brown spots mainly in the throat. They are two-lipped (which is a characteristic feature of many of the members of this family), about an inch long and grow on stems from three to ten inches high. The two-lipped effect is a result of a funnel-like, united base with five lobes of two upper and three lower petals.

Leaves are opposite, sessile (without a petiole), and broadly ovate. Leaves and stems may be used for greens.

The name monkeyflower is from the similarity of masks worn by comics on the early stage.

ELEPHANTELLA

Pedicularis groenlandica   Figwort family

Never has a flower so closely resembled its name-sake than does elephanthead. The name "elephantella" means "little elephant" and is in reference to the elephant head-like flower. The dense spikes of flowers are commonly reddish-purple but may occasionally be pink-rose in some stands. The entire flower stalk usually stands ten to fourteen inches tall in moist open meadows. Along with marsh marigold, elephantella is one of the dominant wild flowers of these moist areas during July.

Close inspection of an individual flower shows the typical two-lipped pattern of the Figwort family. The upper lip is the elephant's trunk with its elongated projecting arch and the lower lip is divided into three parts—two cheeks and the protruding lower lip of the elephant's head.

Leaves are finely dissected, appearing fern-like and arising mainly from the base of the stem.

Elephantella is one of the more easily recognized and remembered Colorado flowers because it is so distinctive in its shape.

Monkeyflower

Elephantella

BRACTED LOUSEWORT

Pedicularis bracteosa var. *paysoniana*   Figwort family

Compacted yellow flowers borne along a flowering spike-like stalk which may be a foot or more long. The entire plant when in full bloom may be two to three feet tall. The floral bloom is progressive up the stalk with the first flowers appearing at the base of the floral axis. The light yellow flowers are interspersed with bracts (small leaf-like structures which subtend the flowers). An individual flower is two lipped with the upper lip forming an arched hood.

Lousewort may also be recognized by its dissected fern-like leaves and sturdy one to two foot floral stalks. As many as eight or ten such floral spikes may grow from an individual plant. They are found in open forested areas or at the edge of meadows mainly in the Subalpine zone during July.

For those readers interested in the genera, there are five very common and showy members of this genus in western Colorado. Each is quite different from the other unless one is looking for the family similarities. They are: *P. groenlandica*, *P. racemosa*, *P. crenulata*, *P. scopulorum* and *P. bracteosa*. Other species are present but less common.

In ancient times seeds of *Pedicularis* were used to kill lice, thus the name of lousewort for a number of genera with this Latin name [*Pedicularis*].

PARROTS-BEAK, SICKLETOP PEDICULARIS

Pedicularis racemosa   Figwort family

Very common in clumps in partial shade of spruce at the Subalpine zone. Unfortunately, it is not as showy as many other wildflowers partially because it is generally in the dense shade of the spruce and partially because of the dull white to cream-colored spike of flowers terminated on stems averaging ten to twelve inches high. From each plant a cluster of five to eight stems may arise but some of these become more or less decumbent.

Flowers of parrots-beak or sickletop pedicularis are quite distinctive and could never be confused with any other of the genus *Pedicularis*. Since this plant is in the Figwort family, the flower is two-lipped with three lobes of the five fused petals making a slightly twisted lower lip and the upper two petals fused into a high curved and pointed sickle or arched parrots beak. It is the nature of the pointed, arched upper two fused petals that has given the common name to this plant; but other names applied to it include ramshorn, mountain figwort and woodbetony.

Leaves are lanceolate (long and narrow) with doubly crenate margins. They arise alternately along the stem.

A peculiarity of the parrots-beak inflorescence is the spiral arrangement of the blossoms when one looks down on top of the floral head.

Bracted Lousewort

Parrots-Beak

PURPLE LOUSEWORT

Pedicularis crenulata   Figwort family

At least two different origins for the name of the genus *Pedicularis* have been suggested. One states that in ancient times seeds were used to kill lice. The other says that where certain species grew abundantly in open meadows in Europe, the cattle grazing there had lice.

Colorado West has several prominent louseworts, each with their distinctive design for the floral "beak". Purple lousewort or meadow pedicularis has a beautiful dark rose-purple blossom with many flowers crowded at the apex in a dense spike. The two upper united petals form an arch (the beak) above the three united lower petals. All five petals are tubular below.

Leaves are distinctively crenate (margins with teeth rounded at the apex) and alternate.

Look for purple lousewort in open moist meadows of the higher mountains. Perhaps the other name of meadow pedicularis would be more appropriate because of its growth habitat.

BUNNY-IN-THE-GRASS
(Lanceleaf Figwort)

Scrophularia lanceolata   Figwort family

A weedy type plant averaging three to four feet in height. These plants are also called bunny-in-the-grass because of the elongated brown to purplish-green flowers with two lips apparently reminded someone of a bunny in the grass. Lanceleaf figworts are common among perennial grasses or on rocky slopes from June to August in Montane zones of western Colorado. Cattle grazing these areas do not touch this figwort so that in these pastured areas it becomes quite conspicuous, not for its flowers but for the tall spindly plant.

The stems are four angled which is commonly a feature of the mint family. But there are a few figwort family members in our territory that may also have this quality. The saw-toothed leaves are opposite on the stem.

The tiny flowers of bunny-in-the-grass have all figwort family characteristics, the united petals form two lips with the upper lip having two erect lobes (the bunny's ears) and the lower lip containing three lobes in a spreading design. There are five stamens in the corolla throat but only four are functional.

Purple Lousewort

Bunny-In-The-Grsss

(Lanceleaf Figwort)

MULLEIN

Verbascum thapsus   Figwort family

Along the gravel edges of the highways of Colorado West at approximately the altitude of the oakbrush zone is a plant which has adapted well to the dry areas of our western United States. Mullein grows throughout the continental United States where precipitation may be abundant or where it is as sparse as our desert and semidesert west. In our area, mullein does well along the roadsides because its root system takes advantage of the extra runoff from the roadway. It is not considered a noxious weed here since it does not invade cultivated areas.

From a cluster of large lanceolate leaves arises a stout two to four foot tall single stem (occasionally with two or three branches). Leaves are also abundant along the axis. These leaves have a soft silver gray appearance because they are densely woolly with branched hairs.

At the tip of this conspicuous stalk is a raceme-type inflorescence which may be a foot long. The yellow five-petaled flowers appear at random along the axis and usually only a few are blooming at any one time. In most racemes the first flowers are at the base of the inflorescence and continued blooming is progressively up the axis. But mullein chose to be unusual.

BEDSTRAW

Galium septentrionale (G. boreale)   Madder family

There are three characteristic features of bedstraw. One of the most obvious is the square stem. The second is the whorled arrangement of the linear to lanceolate leaves on each node. Actually, only two of these are leaves arranged opposite each other; whereas, the other two completing the whorl are the leaflike stipules. The third distinctive feature of bedstraw is the dense cluster of small white terminal flowers. These features are not distinctive of this flower alone but when combined into one flower the combination makes for a quite different flower.

Bedstraw usually stands twelve to fifteen inches high, is common in both open and slightly wooded areas. It is very conspicuous at the Montane and lower Subalpine zones among the oakbrush and aspen regions, but it grows also on bare slopes in road cuts and along highway rights-of-way from July until mid-August. Do not confuse bedstraw with yarrow. Both of these flowers are white and frequently are found together.

Individual flowers have four pointed spreading lobes and four delicate projecting stamens. There are no sepals.

The name bedstraw comes from the old story that the manger of the Christ Child was filled with this plant.

Mullein

Bedstraw

SNOWBERRY

Symphoricarpos oreophilus   Honeysuckle family

Snowberry is a medium sized, delicate looking shrub found crowded among currants and honeysuckles in semi-shaded spruce stands in the Subalpine zone. Leaves are oval to ovate with entire margins. Like other ornamentals in the Honeysuckle family, leaves arise oppositely along the twig.

Flowers are about one-fourth inch long, pendant, light pink and often in pairs. Distinctive features of snowberry are its characteristic twinned pink flowers and opposite leaves. When fruits are present in late summer, white berries become the characteristic feature of the plant.

Another species of *Symphoricarpos* bears light red berries, so logically enough, the bush is called coralberry.

Some individuals know these two shrubs as waxberry or wolfberry. They are grown as ornamentals, appreciated both for their flowers and fruits. The fruits, produced by the cultivated varieties and grown in our yards attract the birds during the winter months.

This family contains several highly-prized ornamentals. Besides snow- and coralberry there is honeysuckle, the Virburnums (arrowwood, wayfaring tree, and cranberry bush), beautybush, weigela, and wild elderberry.

ELDERBERRY

Sambucus melanocarpa   Honeysuckle family

Elderberry is a low shrub with distinctive pinnately compound leaves arranged opposite along the stem. Each leaflet is lanceoltate with pointed tip and serrated margins. The leaflets are also arranged opposite with the terminal leaflet not having a partner. There are usually seven leaflets comprising a single compound leaf.

Flowers and fruits are perhaps the most distinctive features of this plant. From mid-June until late July the shrub is a mass of small white flowers produced at the tips of a much branched inflorescence, called a compound cyme. The entire inflorescence is flat-topped or umbrella shaped depending on the species. An individual flower has five spreading white petals and five stamens. The species common in western Colorado has an inflorescence that is short-pyramidal rather than flat-topped.

The fruits of this particular species are berry-like and turn bright red as they begin to ripen in August and as they reach maturity will dry down and become a dull dirty red. This particular species does not form a dark blue berry contrary to what other sources have indicated. The berries make good food for wildlife in the area but are not sufficiently tasty to be prized by man.

These shrubs can be grown in backyards where they not only produce showy flowers in the spring but attract birds in late fall.

Snowberry

Elderberry fruit

Elderberry flowers

BEARBERRY HONEYSUCKLE

Lonicera involucrata   Honeysuckle family

Like the cultivated form which we grow in our lawn, this wild form is also a shrub with opposite leaves. It is common among large rocks along the roadway and at the edge of dense spruce stands. Honeysuckle or twinflower, as it is called, produces pairs of yellow flowers on short stalks which arise from the axils of twig and leaf. The fused petals are bell-shaped and pendant. The twin flowers are surrounded at their base by four large bracts which are green when the flower is fresh but become reddish and quite showy as the flower begins to fade. Distinctive features then are the opposite leaves, yellow twin flowers and green bracts turning to red.

Fruits are waxy dark purple to black. When matured they are very showy against the background of the red bracts. This fruit is edible but is not particularly tasty.

Our only native honeysuckle in Colorado is well distributed in the western mountainous part of the State at elevations from 7,000 to 11,500 feet.

HAREBELL

Campanula rotundifolia   Bellflower family

This is a delicate slender stemmed plant standing about one foot tall. It prefers open meadows, often found growing next to large rocks.

Bellflower or bluebell would probably be a more appropriate name for this flower. The five fused medium blue petals form a bell which most often is nodding. Occasionally they are quite erect. Outer lobes of the petals form the edge of the bell. They are pointed and make a lovely design at the margins. Most often the flower is solitary but some plants may have two to several "bells" on one stalk.

Stem leaves are small and linear. The stem is so slender that it cannot support much of a leaf!

It is difficult to use the name bluebell for *Campanula* because we already have a common mountain bluebell, *Mertensia*. The latter bluebell has already been referred to under the Borage family members.

Harebells or bluebells are the famous Bluebells of Scotland.

Honeysuckle

Harebell

VALERIAN

Valeriana capitata
and
Valeriana edulis   Valerian family

The word valerian is derived from a Latin word which refers to the medicinal properties of some species of this genus. Here is another instance where a common name was taken from the genus name and for that reason may not have become a household word as have some other native flowers.

Valeriana capitata is common in the Montane and Subalpine zones in mid-summer crowded with the myriads of other flowers in open meadows and along borders of dense wooded areas. The individual flowers are small and white to light pink but in a compacted cluster at the tips of the branches which make a showy one- to two-inch flat-topped spectacle.

Valeriana edulis is the other common valerian in western Colorado. It may be found in the rich soil shaded by spruce (as is *V. capitata*), but it also tolerates very well the open meadows whether of rich deep soil or rocky terrain. *V. edulis* is produced from a taproot and may have several flower stalks arising from the rosette of basal leaves. Flowers are also small, greenish-white and not conspicuous.

A close inspection of one flower of valerian reveals five-lobed petals in a united funnel with three protruding stamens. The smooth stems average from one to three feet tall (depending on the species) with spatulate shaped undivided basal leaves, and two to four pairs of dissected sessile leaves along the stem.

Valerian capitata

Valerian edulis

ASTERS

Machaeranthera canescens
(*Aster rubrotinctus* of manuals)
and
Heterotheca villosa
(*Chrysopsis villosa* of manuals)

Composite or Thistle family

Aster: Since the Composite family is such a large one there are naturally several well known members present among the flora of the western Colorado mountains. Of the fourteen genera selected in this book, asters are one of the more common flowers of this family. There are two types of flowers in this family, and both are present in the aster; one called ray flowers (which we normally call petals) and the other, disc flowers (the large yellow compacted center of the flower). Ray flowers are often white, blue, purple or shades of pink. Disc flowers are usually yellow.

Generally speaking, asters may be separated from daisies by the following characteristics. Asters are usually branched and produce small flowers at the tip of each branch. Second, the ray flowers (petals) are usually less numerous (often less than 30), and wider than in daisy. Third, the involucral bracts which subtend the floral head are not arranged in any set number of rows. They are more imbricated, appearing like shingles on a roof with slight overlap on the base of each bract.

Asters are mid-to late summer flowers and appear to be more numerous in the Oakbrush and Montane zones than in the Subalpine.

Golden Aster: Even though this plant is called golden aster, it does not belong to the genus *Aster* but rather to the genus *Heterotheca*. It does not have genus *Aster* characteristics. This lovely low flower is very common in all of Colorado West in dry environments of road cuts, open meadows, among sage slopes and rocky outcrops ranging from elevations of 4,000 to 10,000 feet. Also, it is conspicuous because it blooms most of the summer.

216

Purple Aster

Golden Aster

DAISY

Erigeron flagellaris
Erigeron speciosus
Erigeron caespitosus   Composite or Thistle family

Daisy is another of the common members of the Composite family and to pick three species from an area as diversified as all of western Colorado is not an easy task. One generally speaks of aster, daisy, pussytoes or coneflower as a single flower when, actually, there may be several hundred flowers forming a composite head. It is this term composite that has become the family name, and the type of inflorescence is the head. Each term is very appropriate. Both ray and disc flowers are irregular and may or may not be showy. When the ray flowers are present they may be white, pink, purple or blue. Disc flowers are yellow.

Since there is such a great similarity of daisy with aster, the general characteristics of the daisy are here given. Usually the daisy is little branched with a single flower terminating each stem. Also the daisy floral head has many narrow rays (petals) and the involucral bracts subtending the head are usually in two even rows, either equal with each other or on two different levels. Bear in mind these are generalities only.

One might compare this discussion with that of aster on the preceding page. The layman often calls many of the composites all daisies or all asters, which ever name is most familiar to them.

The large daisies, *E. speciousus* and *E. caespitosus* are common at higher elevations, particularly the Subalpine zone, while *E. flagellaris* is a conspicuous daisy in the lower Oakbrush zone. Blooming time for the two former named types is late July through August, but *E. flagellaris* mid-June through mid-July.

Daisy flagellaris

Daisy speciosus

Daisy caespitotis

ARNICA

Arnica cordifolia   Composite or Thistle family

Arnica is a perennial composite with ray flowers and disc flowers, both yellow. It has seven to thirteen petal-like outer ray flowers about one inch long and toothed at the tip. The center disc flowers are numerous and tubular. The flower head is usually solitary.

Heartleaf arnica has two to four pairs of stem leaves with the basal pair ovate, heart-shaped at the base, commonly coarsely toothed and long petioled. The uppermost pair of leaves are reduced in size and are not petioled. Opposite leaves aid in distinguishing the arnicas from other yellow flowering composites.

Arnicas are abundant in all of Colorado West mountains, especially around and in small open areas in association with spruce. During mid-July when their bloom is most showy, one could say they are probably surpassed only by dandelion in numbers of plants. Not only do they form large spreading patches at the edges of spruce stands but also around and under aspen trees and at the edge of roadsides.

Broadleaf arnica (*A. latifolia*) is also present in western Colorado. It blooms in early August. Stem leaves are not petioled, or only slightly so, and are more oval rather than heart shaped.

MULES-EARS

Wyethia amplexicaulis   Composite or Thistle family

Some of the plants that look like sunflowers in Colorado West are not really sunflowers. One of the "cousins" is mules-ears, one of the more showy composites that adds to the beauty and blends well with other flowers in its environ. Mules-ears is tall and coarse stemmed with large alternating ovate-lanceolate leaves and flower heads that may be three to four inches across. Both disc and ray flowers are yellow. The ray flowers are what most people call the petals, but each petal really is an entire flower. It is the elongated mule's ear shape of the leaf that gives its name to the flower.

Two other characteristics of the mules-ears are the solitary nature of the flower head and the arrangement of the bracts (located on the underside of the flower head) into two or three rowed series.

This plant is very common in all of western Colorado throughout the Oakbrush zone, blooming in June and early July. Mules-ears are very easy to see from a moving vehicle because of the plant height and large size of the bright yellow-orange flower.

Arnica

Mules-Ears

221

SENECIO, GROUNDSEL

Senecio mutabilis
and
Senecio triangularis   Composite or Thistle family

Rarely does a flowering plant have so many names as does groundsel, senecio, ragwort or butterweed. It probably also indicates the proliferation and variation of the genus in the continental United States in which there are about two hundred species. There are several common species in the western part of our State, but two have been selected as representative of the type; one *S. mutabilis*, blooming in mid-July on upper slopes and the other *S. triangularis*, blooming in the Subalpine zone in late July and early August.

Flower heads are many and small but clustered together to make a showy yellow inflorescence. Ray flowers form the yellow "petals" and the disc flowers, crowded together in the middle, make up the center of the flower. Actually, there are several hundred individual irregular flowers in each flower head. This is typical of the Composite family.

Groundsel may be recognized by tilting a flower head to observe the bell-shaped single series of equal, pointed bracts with a few small bractlets at the base. The seeds are tipped with many soft, white, slender hairs (pappus).

YARROW

Achillea lanulosa   Composite or Thistle family

Yarrow is one of our more familiar mountain wildflowers and one that blooms for a greater part of the summer. Yarrow's distinctive features are the flat-topped cluster of many small white flowers and the finely dissected fern-like leaves. The dull green appearance of the leaves and stems is due to dense hairs. Yarrow is one of those plants which produces a strong odor, especially pronounced if the leaves or stems are crushed or squeezed.

Achillea, the generic name, is in honor of Achilles. According to legend he was the first to have utilized the plant's curative powers.

Yarrow prefers open meadows and roadsides. It has a fondness for the gravelly and sandy well-drained dry areas and for that reason is common on the heavily grazed lower slopes of the forested mountains. However, it is abundant almost everywhere in the State from upper Oakbrush zone to Subalpine.

In places a pink variety appears in late July and August. It is not common but is an interesting varient of the white.

A cultivated perennial, yarrow may also be grown in home flower gardens.

Groundsel mutabilis

Groundsel triangularis

Yarrow

PUSSYTOES

Antennaria rosea   Composite or Thistle family

Also known as catspaw or everlasting, this common but inconspicuous plant looks like little balls of fur. Perhaps to the person who gave it this common name it resembled the toes of a kitten. The clusters of small white or pink flowers forming the flower head are borne on short stems about four to six inches high. In order to find this flower you will have to look closely in open meadows, especially where vegetation is low and sparse. Pussytoes is not a plant that can compete with tall vegetation. It prefers well drained areas or may even thrive among rocks where soil is thin.

Pussytoes belongs to the Composite family (aster or sunflower family) which characteristically has many small inconspicuous flowers tightly compacted into a head. The flowers are of two kinds, male and female, but the male flowers are not common. In this genus the white or pink of the flower is not from petals but from the enlarged upper bracts subtending the flower head. The stems and leaves are very hairy, which gives the leaves a pale green to silvery cast.

Pussytoes begins blooming in our mountains in early to mid-summer and continues through early August. Both the white and pink flowering forms are present but white pussytoes is more abundant.

LITTLE SUNFLOWER

Helianthella quinquenervis   Composite or Thistle family

Little Sunflower is often confused with the common sunflower (*Healianthus*) because the blossoms and coarseness of the leaves are quite similar. Most of the difference between these two flowers are in the detailed features of the flower head and the developing seeds. But there is one external feature that is helpful in field identification. Our species of little sunflower has ovate-lanceolate leaves while the common sunflower has a broadly ovate to deltoid leaf pattern.

Like most of our Colorado mountain composites, little sunflower has a ring of outer ray flowers (yellow) and numerous small disc flowers (darker yellow to slightly brownish, depending on age). Flowers are two to three inches across and usually borne solitary on the stem. Just as in other sunflowers, these flower heads almost invariably face the east.

Basal leaves are numerous and arise from a petiole while the stem leaves arise on the axis and often become smaller toward the top.

The fruits (achenes) are strongly compressed, notched and bear two scaly awns.

This species is restricted to the Subalpine zone of western Colorado. In some of the higher mountain open meadows by late July and early August, little sunflower, lupine, loveroot, geranium, polymonium and scarlet gilia, to list only a few, will produce a fantastic view to those of us who love our mountains.

Pussytoes

Little Sunflower

CONEFLOWER

Rudbeckia occidentalis   Composite or Thistle family

Coneflower is in the Composite family (sunflower family). This species is unlike many of the common members of the family in that it does not have conspicuous ray flowers and, therefore, is not showy. The elongated, conelike, usually solitary flower head is dark brown or black.

A close inspection of this peculiar wildflower shows a ring of green bracts (involucres) subtending the elongated black flower head. All of this conelike structure consists of tiny disc flowers, each with its petals, stamens and pistil. All of these floral parts have this same dark color.

It is not because of its beauty as a delicate wildflower that this plant has been added to the collection, but rather because of its unusual nature. Many persons are of the opinion that this flower is still in the bud or that it has already produced seeds, when actually it is in full bloom.

The entire plant may be three to four feet tall and is commonly found in open areas, especially where cattle have heavily grazed the grass. It is most common in Oakbrush and Montane zones and blooms in late July and into August.

SNEEZEWEED

Dugaldia hoopesii (Helenium hoopesii)   Composite or Thistle family

This flower is certainly one of the more showy of the Composite family. Clumps of sneezeweed start blooming in open meadows and along roadsides in mid-July and persist until September. Along the slopes of the Montane zone it may be in bloom by the latter part of June. Like many Composites it is not particular about the soil thickness or type, so roadside gravels suit it well. And, since this is a relatively tall plant (approximately 18 inches tall), the traveler notices it while driving leisurely along the highway.

The name of sneezeweed is quite appropriate. If there is anyone in your car who is allergic to a variety of plants, sneezeweed might better be looked at than picked and placed in the vehicle.

Disc flowers, the center part of the flower, are most frequently orange but in some plants they may appear reddish-orange. Petals of the ray flowers are bright orange and often one and a half inch long. In most cases these petals tend to droop somewhat, giving a slightly wilted appearance. The bright color and size contribute to the showiness of the flower.

Coneflower

Sneezeweed

GOLDENEYE

Heliomeris multiflora
(Viguiera multiflora of manuals)   Composite or Thistle family

Of all the plant families in the mountainous areas of western Colorado and those displayed in this book, the Composite family has more representatives than any other. And goldeneye is another wildflower of this family. Like most of the members of this family it is very showy. The plant is much branched with sunflower like flowers, an inch or more across, produced at the tips of the branches. Flower heads are bright yellow with the ray flowers producing most of the color. The many center disc flowers are a dull yellow and result in the production of a somewhat darker center.

Leaves are linear-lanceolate with three equally prominent veins. Margins are only obscurely toothed and the surface is somewhat hairy. This rough hairiness can be felt if one rubs a finger over the upper surface.

Look for goldeneye in dry open sunny locations, particularly along the upper flanks of the Oakbrush zone, the entire Montane zone and even well into the Subalpine zone. They are particularly common along the dry roadcuts, thus are readily observed from the auto.

The entire plant stands one and one-half to two feet high. It is a perennial and blooms in late July through August.

THISTLE

Cirscium scopulorum (white)
and
Carduus leiophyllus (pink)
(Carduus nutans)   Composite or Thistle family

Thistle are so common throughout the United States that it could be a flower of any color or a plant of any size and we could recognize it for what it is. Obviously, they are not picked but rather admired from a distance. They can be beautiful and, since they are very common along the roadsides both in the lower and upper vegetative zones during mid-summer, they really should deserve a place in a wildflower collection.

Most everyone recognizes the projected and very pointed spines at the tips of each pinnate lobe of the leaf and along the stem, but perhaps we fail to notice that the white, pink or deep rose of the flower head represents several hundred individual flowers. The tubular corollas of the disc flowers (so common in the Composite family) are very long and split into narrow divisions. Each one of the thread-like colored sections then represents a portion of a dissected petal.

Goldeneye

White Thistle

Pink Thistle

GOLDENROD

Solidago sparsiflora   Composite or Thistle family

Summertime in the Rockies could not come to a close without the display of goldenrod. This is definitely a fall blooming plant, not just here in the Colorado Rockies but all over the United States. Goldenrod and the thought of "back-to-school" go hand in hand. It is such a popular flower around the United States—there are around 125 species present—that several states have selected it as their state flower. Our nearest state with this floral emblem is Nebraska. Other states are farther east.

Goldenrod is a Composite with yellow disc and ray flowers present in each head. Individual flower heads are small with bracts imbricated in several series. The entire floral cluster is often much branched becoming highly modified racemes, cymes or corymbs. Many goldenrods (including the one pictured) are secund; that is, the flowers arise along one side of the axis.

The goldenrod blooms at approximately the 8,000 to 9,000 foot level and is common along roadcuts. Since it is such a showy floral cluster the bright yellow is quite an eyecatcher.

ALPINE SUNFLOWER

Hymenoxys grandiflora   Sunflower family

Like many members of the Composite family, Alpine sunflower has both disc and ray flowers. They are showy and bright yellow, formed into heads that are usually two inches across. Since the plant is quite wooly, other names applicable for this species are graylocks and old-man-of-the-mountain.

Because of its large blossom and bright color, alpine sunflower is one of the more conspicuous flowers of the Alpine zone. It can be found abundantly on slopes that have more soil (less rocky outcrops) and, therefore, among grasses, sedges and other flowering plants. Alpine sunflower is usually conspicuous because it grows a height of six or eight inches, which, among tundra plants, makes them very showy. Also, all blossoms are oriented southward.

The woolly leaves are finely dissected and narrow. Since this is an alpine composite and especially conspicuous, the amateur should have no trouble separating this particular genus from the multitude of composites found at lower elevations.

Goldenrod

Alpine Sunflower

COLOR GUIDE TO THE WILDFLOWERS

Flowers white to greenish:

sego lily - mariposa lily
yucca
pepperweed
locoweeds
evening promrose
desert phlox
white borage
daisy
aster
desert yarrow
townsendia
false solomonseal
twisted stalk
mountain deathcamas
false hellebore
bog orchid
bistort
umbrella plant
chickweed
globeflower
marsh marigold
alpine anemone
columbine
meadowrue
pennycress - wild candytuft
bittercress
snowball saxifrage
gooseberry
thimbleberry
raspberry
strawberry
serviceberry
peavine
wild hollyhock
cow parsnip
loveroot - lovage
Colorado dogwood
green gentian - monument plant
fendler waterleaf
dusky penstemon

paintbrush
parrots beak - sickle top pedicularis
bedstraw
elderberry
valarian
yarrow
pussytoes
coneflower
thistle

Flowers pink to red:

wild onoin
desert four o'clock
pink beeplant
locoweeds
cactus
desert phlox - pink phlox
paintbrush
desert pink
nodding onoin
fairy slipper
coral root
mountain sorrel
columbine
pink corydalis
rockcress
rosecrown
kingscrown
rose
pink plumes
geranium
checkermallow
fireweed
kinnikinnik
shootingstar
primrose
scarlet gilia
pink gilia

fendler waterleaf
giant hyssop

Flowers pink to red [Cont.]

elephantella
bunny-in-the-grass
snowberry
valarian
daisy
pussytoes
thistle

Flowers yellow to orange:

bladderstem - desert trumpet
yellow beeplant
desert plume
princes plume
locoweeds
poppymallow - globemallow
cactus
desert parsley
yellow borage
golden aster
actinea
desert dandelion
paperflower
goldenweed
wild chrysanthemum
cream tips
gaillardia
dogtooth violet
sulphur flower
pondlily
buttercup
yellow corydalis - goldensmoke
wallflower
whitlow grass
stonecrop
potentilla
goldenbanner - goldenpea
violet
mountain parsley
monkeyflower

bracted lousewort
mullein
honeysuckle
arnica
mulesears
senecia - groundsel
little sunflower
sneezeweed
goldeneye
goldenrod

Flowers blue to purple:

lavender mustard
desert parsley
scorpion weed - wild heliotrope
penstemon
aster
Iris
pasque flower
delphinium
larkspur
columbine
monkshood
sugarbowl
lupine
vetch
flax
violet
fringed gentian
jacobsladder
leafy polemonium
low waterleaf
phacelia - purple pincushion
beebalm - monarda
bluebells - mertensia
dusky penstemon
penstemon
hairbell
daisy
thistle

INDEX

236